LISTENING TO THE BIBLE

Saint Luke Painting The Virgin, by Simon Marmion (c) The British Library Board (Add 71117B).

LISTENING TO
THE BIBLE

The Art of Faithful Biblical Interpretation

CHRISTOPHER BRYAN

With an Appendix on Liturgical Reading by
David Landon

OXFORD
UNIVERSITY PRESS

Oxford University Press is a department of the University of Oxford.
It furthers the University's objective of excellence in research, scholarship,
and education by publishing worldwide.

Oxford   New York
Auckland   Cape Town   Dar es Salaam   Hong Kong   Karachi
Kuala Lumpur   Madrid   Melbourne   Mexico City   Nairobi
New Delhi   Shanghai   Taipei   Toronto

With offices in
Argentina   Austria   Brazil   Chile   Czech Republic   France   Greece
Guatemala   Hungary   Italy   Japan   Poland   Portugal   Singapore
South Korea   Switzerland   Thailand   Turkey   Ukraine   Vietnam

Oxford is a registered trademark of Oxford University Press
in the UK and certain other countries.

Published in the United States of America by
Oxford University Press
198 Madison Avenue, New York, NY 10016

© Oxford University Press 2014

Library of Congress Cataloging-in-Publication Data
Bryan, Christopher, 1935–
Listening to the Bible: the art of faithful Biblical interpretation / Christopher
Bryan; with an appendix on liturgical reading by David Landon.
    pages cm
Includes bibliographical references and index.
ISBN 978–0–19–933659–3 (cloth :alk. paper)   1. Bible—Hermeneutics. I. Title.
BS476.B79 2013
220.601—dc23
2013014196

9 8 7 6 5 4 3 2 1
Printed in the United States of America
on acid-free paper

In memoriam
Donald S. Armentrout
1939–2013
A faithful friend is a strong defense, and he that hath
found such an one hath found a treasure.

CONTENTS

ACKNOWLEDGMENTS

As always in having made a book such as this, small though it is, there are many to whom one is indebted and in many ways—for information, advice, encouragement, proofing, research, resources, and countless other gifts. Here are those of whose generosity to me I am most aware, and I name them simply in alphabetical order: the Right Reverend J. Neil Alexander, Fr. Peter Allen, C.R., Ms. Joan Blocher, Dr. Cynthia Crysdale, Dr. James Dunkly, Dr. John Gatta, the Reverend Dr. Julia Gatta, the Reverend Michael Goldsmith, Dr. Paul Holloway, Mr. James David Jones, the Reverend Dr. Benjamin King, Dr. David Landon, the Reverend Dr. Robert MacSwain, Ms. Marcela Maxfield, Ms. Cynthia Read, the Very Reverend William H. Stafford, and the Reverend Dr. Rebecca Abts Wright. Last but hardly least I must acknowledge Wendy Bryan, who graciously continues to put up with me. And as always, of course, I must point out that however indebted I am to all these good people for what they have given me, I alone am responsible for whatever is wrong with the result.

Christopher Bryan
Saint Mark the Evangelist, 2013

LISTENING TO THE BIBLE

THE DIVISION ▼

SOME YEARS AGO I WAS attending, as was then my habit, the Annual Meeting of the Society of Biblical Literature. Hundreds of biblical scholars were gathered together. As we were coming and going through the entrance to the conference hotel, I noticed a small group of people standing to the side holding placards. "What think ye of Christ? Whose Son is he?" they asked. What fascinated me was the response of the biblical scholars, which was no response at all. Everyone passed by gazing fixedly in some other direction. It seemed that something very embarrassing was happening, and we would really rather not see it.

Yet surely the questions on the placards were reasonable questions to put to a group of biblical scholars—arguably the most high-powered and learned in the land? Ought not biblical scholars to have been interested? Should we not have been engaging the group, as Jesus in the gospel engaged the doctors in the Temple, hearing them and asking them questions? Or should we not (since we, presumably, were the doctors) have been inviting them to engage us? Surely in this avoidance of communication there was food for amusement or irritation, depending, as Jane Austen would have put it, on whether you were in a mood for satire or morality.

Of course we biblical scholars would probably have said that we were busy, and the people with placards were most likely fanatics or lunatics with no desire to ask questions or engage in dialogue anyway. And we might have been right. There is such a thing as picking your fights. I say "we," for did I engage in conversation with the group? No, I did not.

But regardless of those details, and the rights and wrongs of the actual occasion, it does occur to me that the little scene might stand as a parable of the engagement, or rather non-engagement, that throughout the twentieth century and so far into the twenty-first has marked the relationship between much academic biblical study and the church. And by "church" I mean ordinary, faithful people who attend church and ordinary, faithful, non-academic clergy who preach to them. In the twenty-first century the overwhelming majority of clergy in the major Christian denominations, Roman Catholic and Reformed alike, have had some training in scholarly—which for all practical purposes nowadays means, historical-critical—approaches to the Bible. But that critical study seems seldom to inform their preaching. While I would not go so far as a friend of mine who declared, "most Church of England clergy preach as if they were fundamentalists," I can see what she meant. If biblical scholarship has affected their preaching at all, it seems chiefly to have been that it has engendered a reluctance to engage the great central tenets of the Christian faith—the divinity of Christ, the resurrection of Christ, the Triune God. To hear about those things, you perhaps do better if your parish priests or pastors were more interested in patristics or liturgy when they were at theological college or seminary. Yet as James Sanders has reminded us, the true setting-in-life (*sitz im leben*) of the Bible is the community of faith—the synagogue and the church—and always has been.[1] So how can a study of Scripture claim any measure of completeness if it remains unrelated to that setting? How can it claim to be truly "historical critical" or "scientific," if it ignores the context in which and for which those texts were created? Is our scientific investigation "sufficiently scientific"?[2]

Certainly there are in every part of the Christian community notable exceptions to the separation I have been describing. Still, a tendency to divorce is clear. It was remarked on sixty or so years ago by the Anglican C. S. Lewis,[3] a writer and a literary critic who (irritating though some may find it) was also probably the most widely influential apologist for Christianity of the twentieth century.[4] It was remarked on more recently by Marilynne Robinson, among the finest novelists and thinkers of our time.[5] It has been remarked on over several decades by Protestants,[6] Anglicans,[7] and Roman Catholics.[8] Michael Legaspi goes so far as to say that, "the scriptural Bible and the academic Bible are fundamentally different creations oriented toward rival interpretative communities."[9]

All these observers, in one way or another, see the issue as a matter for concern.

How, then, did this come about?

Notes

1. See e.g., James A. Sanders, *From Sacred Story to Sacred Text: Canon as Paradigm* (Philadelphia: Fortress, 1987), 193. I am grateful to my friend and colleague Paul Holloway for drawing my attention to Sanders's reflections.
2. Adrian Walker, "Fundamentalism and the Catholicity of Truth," *Communio* **29** (2002): 21.
3. In his paper, "Modern Theology and Biblical Criticism," in *Christian Reflections*, Walter Hooper, ed. (Grand Rapids, Mich.: Eerdmans, 1967), 152–66; subsequently republished under the title "Fern-seed and Elephants" in *Fern-seed and Elephants and other essays on Christianity by C. S. Lewis*, Walter Hooper, ed. (Glasgow: William Collins, Fontana, 1975), 104–25.
4. See Robert MacSwain, *The Cambridge Companion to C. S. Lewis* (Cambridge University: 2010), 1–4.

5. Marilynne Robinson, *Absence of Mind: The Dispelling of Inwardness from the Modern Myth of the Self* (New Haven: Yale University, 2010), especially 24–29; see also her trenchant observations in "The Fate of Ideas: Moses," in *When I Was a Child I Read Books* (New York: Farrar, Straus and Giroux, 2012), 95–124.
6. E.g., David Steinmetz, "The Superiority of Pre-Critical Exegesis," in *Theology Today 37* (1980), 27–38; also in *Ex auditu 1* (1985), 74–82; Geoffrey Wainwright, "Towards an Ecumenical Hermeneutic: How Can All Christians Read the Scriptures Together?" *Gregorianum 76* (1995) 648–49; R. W. L. Moberly, *The Bible, Theology, and Faith: A Study of Abraham and Jesus* (Cambridge: Cambridge University Press, 2000), 4–5.
7. E.g., Rowan A. Greer, *Anglican Approaches to Scripture* (New York: Herder and Herder, 2006), 171–83; C. FitzSimons Allison, "The Incarnate Word and the Written Word," *Sewanee Theological Review 55*.3 (2012): 279–92.
8. E.g., Joseph Ratzinger (afterwards Benedict XVI), *Schriftauslegung im Widerstreit*, QD 117 (Freiburg im Breisgau: Herder, 1989); Luke Timothy Johnson, *The Real Jesus: The Misguided Quest for the Historical Jesus and the Truth of the Traditional Gospels* (San Francisco: HarperSanFrancisco, 1996); L. John Topel, S. J., "Faith, Exegesis, and Theology," *Irish Theological Quarterly 69* (2004): 337–48; Matthew Levering, *Participatory Biblical Exegesis: A Theology of Biblical Interpretation* (Notre Dame, Ind.: University of Notre Dame Press, 2008), 1–3.
9. Michael Legaspi, *The Death of Scripture and the Rise of Biblical Studies* (Oxford: Oxford University Press, 2010), 169.

HOW DID WE GET HERE? ▼

A CLAIM TO IDENTIFY THE beginnings of any movement is almost always open to challenge, since most of us build whatever we build on foundations laid by others.[1] Still, an early stage of the approach to Scripture that we know as "historical criticism" may reasonably be identified with Friedrich Schleiermacher's Academy Addresses "On the Concept of Hermeneutics," delivered in August 1829.[2] Schleiermacher said that the primary task of the interpreter was to avoid misunderstanding and to discover the author's intent. This was true of interpreting the Bible as of any other word, written or spoken: "I wish to explore how my friend has moved from one thought to another or try to trace out the views, judgments, and aspirations which led him to speak in this way about a given subject and no other."[3] Therefore, contrary to what many had previously thought, a sound approach to understanding the Bible could not distinguish different kinds of interpretation, such as "dogmatic" or "allegorical," to be placed over against the "grammatical-historical,"[4] since in a given piece there could not be "various kinds of interpretation from which interpreters can freely choose." There could only be the meaning the author intended. What was needed, then, for sound interpretation of a text was that Scriptural interpretation, "starting from the simple fact of understanding by reference to the nature of language and by the fundamental conditions relating to a writer and reader or a speaker and hearer, should develop its rules into a systematic, self-contained discipline."[5]

One has only to read Benjamin Jowett's essay, "On the Interpretation of Scripture," published in 1860, to sense the early excitement and confidence that such proposals generated. Jowett, an ardent and (for England) early advocate of the historical critical method, was as clear as Schleiermacher about the basic work of the interpreter. It was a first principle "that Scripture has but one meaning—the meaning which it had to the mind of the Prophet or Evangelist who first uttered or wrote, to the hearers or readers who first received it."[6] Hence, the teachings of the Christian church, which related the Scriptures to the debates and doctrines of later ages, were not an aid to understanding the Bible but a roadblock to it. We needed to "free our minds from the illusion that the Apostle or Evangelist must have written with a reference to the creeds or controversies or circumstances of other times."[7] We needed to abandon both "the attempt to adapt the truths of Scripture to the doctrines of the creeds" and also "the adaptation of the precepts and maxims of Scripture to the language of our own age."[8] Insisting that Scripture address our own concerns and controversies resulted in "an unfair appropriation of some portions of Scripture and an undue neglect of others...What men have brought to the text they have also found there."[9] Clear and exact methods of Enlightenment thinking and investigation, which would lead in turn to clear and exact answers to our questions, demanded of us that we interpret the Scripture not in the light of some predetermined ecclesiastically based faith, but "like any other book. There are many respects in which the Scripture is unlike any other book; these will appear in the results of such an interpretation."[10]

Jowett's essay caused a furor when it was published. Yet the furor passed, and within decades what was initially regarded in Britain and North America as revolutionary was accepted in universities and seminaries as normal. It is amazing how far the world of scholarship came in such a short time.

Undoubtedly, good things were achieved by the approach that Schleiermacher and Jowett advocated. Cobwebs and grime were removed from many pages of Scripture, and things that had been hidden or obscure were revealed. Who would want to be without the improvements to our text that have resulted from the painstaking work of B. F. Westcott and F. J. A. Hort and their successors? Who would want to be without our awareness of Markan primacy, and the ways in which through it we can see not only the brilliance of Mark's original narrative construction, but also the particular theological concerns that led Matthew and Luke to revise him? Who would wish to go back to a situation in which the peculiar concerns and thinking of Saint Paul or the fourth evangelist were ignored? Who would want to lose the deepening study of rabbinic and other Jewish sources that marked the twentieth century?—and in particular, who would want to be without the Qumran discoveries, and all we may learn from them of the text and early understandings of Israel's Scripture, of the evolution of Israel's faith and practice, and through those things of the world into which Christianity was born? Who would want to lose all that has been gained from analyzing the socio-cultural settings of the early Christian communities and, hence, of the New Testament? Who would want to be without the insights into our texts that can emerge from the study of ancient rhetoric?

And yet, even as we revel in these successes, we hesitate. For despite them all, it seems to many even within the discipline of biblical scholarship that something has gone wrong.

I still recall my keen disappointment, and even distress, when as a student I turned from the English language and literature school at Oxford to the theological school. There I found that in contrast with what we were doing with poets and novelists in the English school—and, incidentally, in contrast with what I had earlier learned at grammar school from my first teacher of English literature, the poet T. E. Blackburn—in the theological school we seemed not so much concerned with learning how to listen to our texts for what they had to say to us, as with dissecting them for some hypothetical source or situation or information that might lie behind them.[11] Nor did subsequent experience over the next forty or so years entirely falsify that impression. To pursue the metaphor, instead of stripping off cobwebs and grime to reveal the pages, much scholarly effort seemed concerned to dissect the binding and take apart the pages themselves, being determined not merely to be free from church decrees, as Jowett wished, but also from the texts themselves, preferring to go behind them and then to interpret other "texts" and "sources" that were more "original" than the *actual* texts and that would therefore teach us what "really" happened and show us the "real" Jesus of history. The Jesus Seminar toward the end of the twentieth century provided an extreme but by no means isolated example of such scholarship. This is manifestly not to listen to the biblical texts in any serious sense at all. It is to construct our own text, which is often unconcerned with, or even openly dismissive of, the very issue that in fact unites all the texts of Old and New Testaments: that is, the question of God.

Even, for the sake of argument, leaving aside theological questions, the dangers of such "source" criticism and its "reconstruction" of alleged "sources" that do not in fact

exist are obvious, as we can see from cases where we do
have an author's source. Thus, a main source for Josephus
in his *Antiquities of the Jews* was evidently Israel's scripture: a passage such as *Antiquities* 2:281-287 is obviously
based on Exodus 7:8-12. But what if we did *not* possess this
particular source, if we only had the text of the *Antiquities*?
Then, as Richard I. Pervo points out, while scholars could
possibly imagine a source containing a story about "an
Egyptian king who challenged Moses to a contest with
his own magicians, whose trick of transforming rods into
serpents was trumped by Moses," and while Josephus's
own additions, like "the little speech contrasting divine
reality to deceiving appearances" might be "detectable,"
still, "not even a source critic learned in all the wisdom
of the Egyptians could, from this passage alone, detect
the absence of Aaron."[12] And that is the problem of working with, or still worse, building theories upon, "recon-
structed" sources that do not exist.

Historical-criticism, as I have said, started out with
high hopes. Precise questions were to be asked, and then
followed through with scientific precision so as to deliver
clear answers. In the event, practice of the discipline now
has quite a long history, and we can see from it that to
many—perhaps most—of our important questions it has
not delivered anything like clear answers. On the contrary,
its adepts have created a dark forest of hypotheses that few
ordinary Christians, indeed few ordinary people, wish to
enter. Northrop Frye, writing not as a theologian nor even
especially as a churchman, but rather as a literary critic,
expressed his frustration over this: "textual scholarship has
never really developed the 'higher' criticism that made such
a noise in the nineteenth century. Instead of emerging from

lower criticism, or textual study, most of it dug itself into a still lower, or sub-basement, criticism in which disintegrating the text became an end in itself. As a result its essential discoveries were made quite early, and were followed by a good deal of straw-thrashing."[13] Markus Bockmuehl sees the problem as within the discipline:

> Strange as it sounds, an outside observer today would be hard put to identify *any shared purpose or subject matter* for the discipline whose transactions are chronicled in *New Testament Abstracts* for the twenty first century. Never mind assured facts, methods, or meanings: is there even an identifiable field of study?...
>
> Judging from *New Testament Abstracts*, is the primary object of this study (1) the exegesis and subject matter of the New Testament texts themselves (2) the power interests to which those texts are or can be turned, or (3) the ancient Jewish and Greco-Roman social world, of which the texts formed but an insignificant part? And if one's work is primarily or exclusively on the second or third objects, does it matter for the subject definition if such pursuit still recognizably relates to the first?...It is by no means clear that New Testament studies as an academic discipline now manifests anything approaching a consensus about even its purpose and object.[14]

Surely there is an element of hyperbole in all this: yet one can see why Frye and Bockmuehl write as they do. There *is* a great deal of confusion—which is not going to go away, at least not in the immediate future. No doubt there are many reasons for this, but two of them surely lie in the academic project itself, at least as Jowett and others conceived it.

I consider these in my next chapter.

Notes

1. George Steiner suggests that a historical relativism that will admit no beginnings at all "could be spurious hindsight," and points to exceptions in "the quality of genius in the Greek and Hebraic statement of human possibility, the fact that no subsequent articulation of felt life in Western tradition has been either as complete or as formally inventive" (*After Babel* [Oxford: Oxford University Press, 1975], 19–20). I find this persuasive, and would press it further: but in any case I am not claiming that the rise of historical criticism represents such a beginning.

2. Friedrich Schleiermacher, *Hermeneutics: the handwritten manuscripts*, Heinz Kimmerle, ed., James Duke and Jack Forstman, transl. (Missoula, Mont.: Scholars, 1977), 175–214.

3. Schleiermacher, *Hermeneutics*, 181–82.

4. Schleiermacher, *Hermeneutics*, 213.

5. Schleiermacher, *Hermeneutics*, 214 (Duke and Forstman's translation corrected).

6. Benjamin Jowett, "On the Interpretation of Scripture," in *Essays and Reviews*, 8th ed. (London: Longman, Green, Longman and Roberts, 1861), 378.

7. Jowett, "Interpretation," 334.

8. Jowett, "Interpretation," 353–54.

9. Jowett, "Interpretation," 358–59.

10. Jowett, "Interpretation," 377.

11. See Christopher Bryan, "C. S. Lewis as a Reader of Scripture," in *A Sewanee Companion to "The Cambridge Companion to C. S. Lewis,"* Robert MacSwain, ed., STR 55.2 (Sewanee, Tenn.: University of the South, 2012): 180–207; also online at http://christopherbryanonline.com/articles/cs-lewis-and-the-bible/.

12. Richard I. Pervo, *Dating Acts: Between the Evangelists and the Apologists* (Santa Rosa: Polebridge, 2006) 6–7. Pervo therefore writes modestly of his work on Acts, "Without doubting that Luke made use of oral traditions and other sources, I, who fall far short of mastery of all the wisdom of the Egyptians and a

great deal else, shall not here make a general attempt to recon-
struct them" (op. cit. 11).

13. Northrop Frye, *The Great Code: The Bible and Literature* (San
    Diego: Harcourt, 1981), xvii.
14. Markus Bockmuehl, *Seeing the Word: Refocusing New
    Testament Study* (Grand Rapids, Mich.: Baker Academic,
    2006), 38, 39.

III

WHY JOWETT'S PROJECT

WAS IMPOSSIBLE

WILHELM DILTHEY (1833–1911), THE GERMAN philosopher of history and culture, who was much inspired by
Schleiermacher's work and helped to make it known, was
also one who early saw a snag in it. Dilthey spoke of "the hermeneutical circle," by which he indicated that total objectivity in an inquiry is not possible for us, because even by what
we choose as our starting point, asking one question rather
than another, we unavoidably bring into the inquiry some of
our own assumptions about what is or is not important or
appropriate.[1] Certainly (as Dilthey was aware) distinctions
can be made. Enlightenment methods of detached, "objective" inquiry do have some measure of success in producing
clear answers when applied in the area of the natural sciences
(*Naturwissenschaften*[2]), where experiments can be repeated
and results verified. I say *some* measure of success, for even
here, Heisenberg's Uncertainty Principle (in brief, that an
observer cannot assign exact simultaneous values to the
position and to the momentum of a physical system) makes
us aware of the general truth that the subject conducting
the inquiry always affects the result of the inquiry, and the
fact of the inquiry itself is something that has to be factored
into any inquiry, and so on, ad infinitum.[3] In other words,
in the human field of operations there is no such thing as a
purely detached or objective approach to anything. If scien-
tists remind themselves of such things even in the realm of
natural science, how much more we need to remember them

in the realm of the human sciences (*Geisteswissenschaften*), concerned with events where experiments cannot be repeated and results cannot be verified. We are always, as Marilynne Robinson puts it, "that mysterious presence, the Observer, who can never wholly stand apart from the object of inquiry."[4]

In the light of all this, then, we need hardly be surprised that historical criticism did not turn out to be the panacea that its first proponents expected. Jowett said of pre-Enlightenment biblical study that "What men have brought to the text they have also found there," and no doubt he was right. But in the century and a half after Jowett the situation did not change, for historical critical method was no more able to protect its practitioners from writing under the influence of their own prejudices and interests than were the methods that preceded it. Schleiermacher himself provided an example of this, for his conviction that positive historical revelation was of the very essence of the Christian faith, and that the essential historical facts for that revelation were to be found in the inner being and consciousness of Jesus, surely contributed not only to his predilection for the fourth gospel as a historical source but also to his conviction that Jesus suffered only *Scheintod* ("apparent death," "suspended animation") on the cross, since external events such as Jesus' death and resurrection could be no part of his inner being and consciousness, and therefore no part of the revelation.[5]

Three later examples from the history of such criticism will serve, however, to illustrate this further.

First, scholarly claims to be dealing with "Judaism versus Hellenism" over the last two hundred or so years repeatedly turn out on investigation to have been (consciously or unconsciously) covers for quite different projects. These

include attempts by German intellectuals early in the nineteenth century to rally support for German nationalism and
German Liberal Protestantism against Roman Catholicism,[6]
the attempt by Matthew Arnold in the late nineteenth century to urge a turning by the English middle class from
overly serious, ethical, bourgeois values to those of reflection, high culture, and "sweetness and light,"[7] and attempts
by post-Holocaust American intellectuals in the fifties and
sixties to find an escape from their dominant cultural *angst*
over the fractured state of modernity, trapped in a history
that was timeless because it was meaningless.[8] Naturally,
each project read into "Judaism" and "Hellenism" the particular characteristics that were important for its own proceed-
ing. For the early nineteenth century Germans, "Hellenism"
(good) stood for the universal, for the rational, and for valu-
ing the "independent self-consciousness," as opposed to
"Judaism" (bad), which was cramped and narrowing, rely-
ing on "outward authority" and the "Mother Church."[9] For
Matthew Arnold, "Judaism" ("Hebraism") (good if kept
in proportion) stood for action, ethics, and conscience, as
opposed to "Hellenism" (also good if kept in proportion),
which stood for thinking, knowing, and spontaneity of consciousness.[10] For mid-twentieth-century post-Holocaust
Americans, "Hellenism" (bad) stood for a cyclic, "static"
view of time, for culture, and for individualism, as opposed
to "Judaism" (good), which stood for a "linear" view of history, for "Christ against culture," and for "corporate solidar-
ity."[11] Such a history has produced its own ironies, one such
being that whereas "European asceticism" (good) was cred-
ited by the Jewish poet Heine in the early nineteenth century
to "Judaism" (also good), the post-Holocaust Americans, *dis-
approving* of asceticism, attributed it to "Hellenism" (bad),

contrasting it with "Judaism's positive evaluation of the body and of sexuality."[12]

Second, and in some respects nearer to home: a number of studies written in the last decade or so purport to deal with the Roman Empire in its relationships to Judaism and Christianity. Yet it is evident even to a quite casual reader that what these studies have *actually* been dealing with is the authors' discomfort with contemporary American imperialism in *its* relationships to the rest of the world.[13] Such discomfort may or may not be well-founded, but to argue for it by applying to second-century Rome—even, as is sometimes the case, with immense learning and ingenuity—ideals and ideologies that are manifestly not merely post-second century but post-Enlightenment and even post-colonial, and in terms of which *no* ancient polity would come off well, is no way either to promote justice or to write history.[14]

I am aware, of course, that there is a long and perfectly respectable tradition in letters of dealing with something in the present while pretending to deal with something in the past. One thinks of John Dryden's *Absalom and Achitophel*, published in 1681. On the surface it retold the biblical story; in reality it was a satirical attack on Lord Shaftesbury's attempt to exclude the Duke of York from the English succession and replace him by the Duke of Monmouth. The difference, however, was this: in the case of *Absalom and Achitophel*, everyone, friend and foe alike, knew exactly what was going on. In our contemporary "Roman histories," despite the great learning and ingenuity to which I have referred, I am not at all sure that everyone *does* know what is going on, including those who write them.

Thirdly, and most important of all, is the variety of approaches to the figure of Jesus himself that have emerged from ostensibly objective "historical" study over the last century or so. Here, perhaps more than anywhere else, it is clear that "what men brought to the text they also found there"; or, to put it another way, it is clear that historical-critical scholars, however objective they may have claimed to be or thought they were being, have been unable to resist the temptation to create a Jesus who is in their own image. So, as George Tyrrell pointed out as early as 1910, when Liberal Protestants looked back at Christ "through nineteen centuries of Catholic darkness," what they saw was "only the reflection of a Liberal Protestant face, seen at the bottom of a deep well."[15] The story of the "quest" (as it came to be known) for "the historical Jesus" throughout the late eighteenth and nineteenth centuries is indeed fascinating. A classic account of it up to the beginning of the twentieth century was written by Albert Schweitzer (1875–1965), *Von Reimarus zu Wrede*, published in 1906, and first made available in an English translation as *The Quest of the Historical Jesus* in 1910. Schweitzer showed, often with biting wit, how each writer's opinion of Jesus' message had been determined by the writer's own philosophical preferences and even more by contemporary understandings of reality. In other words, he pointed to the essentially *subjective* nature of their allegedly *objective* studies. His account is still well worth reading.

Naturally, the story did not end there. The twentieth and twenty-first centuries have seen continuing movements and counter-movements. For a while, received truth in the academy asserted that one could know almost nothing about the historical Jesus (Rudolf Bultmann); then one could know something (Ernst Käsemann); then one could know quite a lot (E. P. Sanders). There was a "new" quest for Jesus, and then there was a "third" quest (though accounts of these quests do not always agree with each other as to which scholar fits where).[16] The Jesus discovered by these quests was many things (sometimes incompatible with each other, but not always): he was a pious *hasid* (Geza Vermes; Marcus Borg[17]); he was a social reformer and revolutionary (Richard Horsley[18]); he was a wandering cynic sage (Burton Mack, John Dominic Crossan, F. Gerald Downing[19]); he was an eschatological prophet (E. P. Sanders, John P. Meier, N. T. Wright, J. D. G. Dunn, José A. Pagola[20]).

In other words, scholars of different philosophical and religious persuasions continued throughout the twentieth and into the twenty-first century, just as in the nineteenth, to discover a Jesus consonant with their own hopes and convictions. Seventy or so years after publication of Schweitzer's *Quest*, the Jesus of the Jesus Seminar[21] was an "enigmatic sage," a model of late-twentieth-century political correctness who would be quite at home in the North American divinity schools that created him. With pleasing though presumably unconscious irony, the Seminar declared as a "final general rule of evidence," "Beware of finding a Jesus who is entirely congenial to you."[22] Perhaps they thought to address the churches and meant, "Beware of finding a Jesus congenial to catholic and evangelical religion." I cannot be sure. But they did seem to find a Jesus entirely congenial to themselves.[23]

Of course, Jesus scholarship is not the only kind of scholarship to have created autobiography when it professed to be creating biography: a glance at the plethora of "lives" of Shakespeare that have been written since the early nineteenth century would be enough to illustrate that[24]—not to mention those of proposed "real authors" of Shakespeare's work such as Edward de Vere.[25] But Jesus scholarship has certainly contributed more than its share of such reflection

and—this is my point—it has done so as much when it osten-
tatiously claimed "objectivity" as when it admitted to a basis
in Christian faith. There is, no doubt, a streak of Malvolio
in all of us, always inclined to make the evidence "resemble
something in me"—or at least some fancy of ours—if we
possibly can.

A second problem with the hermeneutical process as
Schleiermacher and his followers conceived it is that their
proposals vastly oversimplified and underestimated what
is actually involved in *any* act of communication and comprehension—let alone a communication between past and
present, the ancient and the modern. As George Steiner
has shown us, even for an Anglophone reader encountering English texts written since 1800, any thorough reading
of any piece of language or literature is "a manifold act of
interpretation," for "language is in perpetual change."[26] If that
is how things are within such a limited range of cultural and
linguistic development, how very much more complex is the
problem that faces a modern reader encountering texts in an
ancient language from the ancient world! The whole thing is
too big, too complex, and too swiftly changing for any group
of precise questions to be devised that could look for precise answers. This is not to despair of interpreting ancient
texts: it is simply to concede that "every language act has a
temporal determinant," and that the range of possibilities
that might actually be explored—semantic, cultural, historical, personal—in order to assure full comprehension of
almost any statement by anyone at all approaches infinity.[27]
Biblical interpretation, like all other interpretation, will be
aided by research—by asking as many "precise questions" as
possible: but it must in the end be a matter of art and imagination, not of science.

Notes

1. Wilhelm Dilthey, *Selected Writings*, ed. H. P. Rickman (Cambridge: Cambridge University, 1976), 259–262. On Dilthey in context see Andrew Louth's now classic study, *Discerning the Mystery: An Essay on the Nature of Theology* (Oxford: Clarendon, 1983), 1–26 and especially 17–26.

2. While much of the intellectual and practical tradition that now comprises "science" is old, the category of "science" itself is relatively new. Prior to the nineteenth century, there was no standard, collective term for it: the German word that would come to mean "science," *Naturwissenschaft*, was a somewhat vague term with various possible meanings and synonyms. By 1850, however, it was generally used in the sense that we associate with it: see Denise Phillips, *Acolytes of Nature: Defining Natural Science in Germany, 1770–1850* (University of Chicago Press, 2012).

3. Werner Heisenberg, *Physics and philosophy: the revolution in modern science* (New York: Harper and Row, 1962).

4. Marilynne Robinson, *When I was a Child I Read Books* (New York: Farrar, Strauss and Giroux, 2012), 57.

5. Schleiermacher, "Einleitung ins neue Testament," in *Sämmtliche Werke*, I.8.218.

6. See Dale B. Martin, "Paul and the Judaism/Hellenism Dichotomy" in *Paul Beyond the Judaism/Hellenism Divide*, Troels Engberg-Pedersen, ed. (Louisville: Westminster John Knox, 2001), 33–44; cf. Philip S. Alexander, "Hellenism and Hellenization as Problematic Historiographical Categories," op. cit. 63–80.

7. Martin, "Dichotomy," 48–49.

8. Martin, "Dichotomy," 50–52.

9. Martin, "Dichotomy," 33–34.

10. Martin, "Dichotomy," 49.

11. Martin, "Dichotomy," 51, 52.

12. Martin, "Dichotomy," 48.

13. E.g., Richard Horsley, *Jesus and Empire: The Kingdom of God and the New World Disorder* (Minneapolis: Fortress, 2003).

14. See generally the writings of Richard Horsley, Richard J. Cassidy, and Warren Carter; for critique see Christopher Bryan, *Render to Caesar: Jesus, the Early Church, and the Roman Superpower* (New York: Oxford, 2005) esp. 3–10, 113–30.
15. George Tyrrell, *Christianity at the Crossroads* (London and New York: Longmans, Green and Company, 1910), 44.
16. For accounts, see N. T. Wright, *Jesus and the Victory of God* (London: S.P.C.K. / Minneapolis: Fortress, 1996), 13–124; Gerd Theissen and Annette Merz, *The Historical Jesus: A Comprehensive Guide* (Philadelphia: Fortress, 1998), 1–16.
17. Geza Vermes, *Jesus the Jew: A Historian's Reading of the Gospels* (London: Collins, 1973); Marcus Borg, *Jesus: Uncovering the Life, Teachings, and Relevance of a Religious Revolutionary* (New York: HarperCollins, 2006).
18. Richard A. Horsley, *Jesus and Empire: The Kingdom of God and the New World Order* (Minneapolis: Fortress, 2003).
19. Burton Mack, *A Myth of Innocence: Mark and Christian Origins* (Philadelphia: Fortress, 1988); John Dominic Crossan, *The Historical Jesus: The Life of a Mediterranean Jewish Peasant* (San Francisco: HarperCollins / Edinburgh: T. & T. Clark, 1991); F. Gerald Downing, *Cynics and Christian Origins* (Edinburgh: T. & T. Clark, 1992).
20. E. P. Sanders, *Jesus and Judaism* (Philadelphia: Fortress, 1985; John P. Meier, *A Marginal Jew; Rethinking the Historical Jesus.* 4 vols. (Anchor/Yale, 1991-2009); N. T. Wright, *Jesus and the Victory of God* (London: S.P.C.K. / Minneapolis: Fortress, 1996; J. D. G. Dunn, *Jesus Remembered* (Grand Rapids, Mich. / Cambridge, England: Eerdmans, 2003); José A. Pagola, *Jesus: A Historical Approximation* (Miami, Fla.: Convivium, 2009).
21. For discussion of the Jesus Seminar, see Luke Timothy Johnson, *The Real Jesus* (New York: HarperCollinsSanFrancisco, 1995); Birger A. Pearson, "The Gospel According to the Jesus Seminar" *Religion* **25** (1995), 317–38. Neither of these accounts of the Seminar is particularly flattering: for positive evaluations, see e.g., Robert W. Funk, "The Issue of Jesus" in

Forum 1.1 (March, 1985) 7–12; *The Five Gospels*, R. W. Funk, R. W. Hoover, and the Jesus Seminar, eds. (New York: MacMillan, 1993), 1–2.

22. *The Five Gospels*, 5.
23. John Dominic Crossan, incidentally, writes with admirable self-awareness and openness on these issues: see *A Long Way from Tipperary* xvi-xix.
24. See Graham Holderness, *Nine Lives of William Shakespeare* (London: Continuum, 2011), especially 1–24.
25. See James Shapiro, *Contested Will: Who Wrote Shakespeare?* (New York: Simon and Schuster, 2010).
26. George Steiner, *After Babel* (Oxford: Oxford University Press, 1975), 17.
27. Steiner, *After Babel*, 24 and passim.

IV

THE HERMENEUTIC OF SUSPICION

IN CONNECTION WITH THE FORGOING chapter, I should perhaps say something of that "hermeneutic of suspicion" of whose necessity we have recently heard much talk in the scholarly guild. In one way, of course, "hermeneutic of suspicion" is only a rather tautological way of saying something that thoughtful people have known for a long time, something that is, arguably, implicit in the word "hermeneutic" alone: words may not always mean, or may not only mean, what they appear to mean at first hearing. The delightful scenes of Portia's courtship in Shakespeare's *The Merchant of Venice* depend, of course, on just such awareness—"all that glisters is not gold." All "hermeneutic" ("interpretation") by its nature involves such "suspicion." Those who read "with interpretation" at Ezra's reading of the Law would not have been needed if the Law's meaning had been simply self evident (Neh. 8:8). As Schleiermacher pointed out, "there would be no reason for hermeneutics to begin if nothing were strange between the speaker and the hearer."[1] Some kinds of expression, such as irony and metaphor, and some kinds of understanding, such as the ancient "fourfold sense," *depend* on such suspicion. Members of the audience are *supposed* to be suspicious that something is going on in the text other or deeper than what is apparent on the surface. Part of their task, part of the art of interpretation, is to perceive and enjoy it.

There are also, of course, occasions when we may properly feel such suspicion in a rather different way: as when we suspect that texts, either with intention on the part of their authors or not, are not telling us the truth, or at least not the whole truth. An example of this would be in our reading of narratives from patriarchal societies—which includes all our biblical narratives—in connection with what they tell us of the role played by women. It is a characteristic of such narratives that they do not in general mention the part played by women unless the women's presence is either a problem or in some way remarkable.[2] But that, we must realize, does not mean that women were not there, or that they did not make a contribution. Hence, we are not to be surprised when, in the synoptic gospels, the faithful women turn up at the foot of the cross, having been scarcely mentioned hitherto. They are mentioned now because their presence is remarkable— they are saving the honor of Jesus' followers, since all his male disciples have fled. But they have, in fact, been present all the time, as the synoptic evangelists, in one way or another, all admit (Mark 15:40-41; Matt. 27:55; Luke 8:2-3, 24:59). (Among these, Luke deserves honorable mention in that he does actually speak of the women's service while telling Jesus' story. Mark and Matthew only speak of it when the women's presence at the cross obliges them to do so. Again, it is Luke alone who notes that the women not only accompanied Jesus and his disciples but also "provided for them out of their resources" [Luke 8:3]. In other words, the women bankrolled the operation.) Here then—and especially if we care about justice for women and about properly honoring the gifts that they bring to us—is an area where the hermeneutic of suspicion may be experienced as liberating and enriching, allowing us to open ourselves to the gospel narratives and to appreciate them in ways that were not previously available to us.

Another appropriate place for such suspicion would be treatment of "the Pharisees" in Saint Matthew's gospel and "the Jews" in Saint John's. These treatments have evidently been affected by their communities' histories, which seem to have involved bitter quarrels with the synagogue. As a result, what we are hearing is not simply a record of the relationship of "the Pharisees" and "the Jews" with Jesus, who was, of course, himself a Jew (although not, I think, a Pharisee, as some have suggested). The striking fact is that Matthew and John are among the most obviously *Jewish* texts in the New Testament. What we are hearing, therefore, is the story of Jesus' relationship to his compatriots told in the light of, and from one side of, *a subsequent bitter family quarrel.* We must understand that, we must make the appropriate discount in our listening to the narrative, and above all we must not suppose that we have any right to make that quarrel into our quarrel. We have no part in it. Here, too, and especially if we have Jewish friends whom we admire and love, the hermeneutic of suspicion can be a source of relief and enlightenment.

Such a hermeneutic of suspicion as I have described is deconstructive, but that does not mean that it is destructive. It does not demolish the text, but rather explores what is going on in and around it. When the hermeneutic is complete, the text still stands, and stands more clearly: the gospel narratives have not inspired millions over millennia because of what they said or assumed about the roles of women in society or the relationship between the church and the synagogue, but because of their witness to Jesus Christ. What a deconstructive hermeneutic does, however, is help us to include in our attention issues that might otherwise remain forgotten or suppressed. Hence the *prophetic* role that a properly applied hermeneutic of suspicion may play in our exegesis, enabling us to recognize and name the extent to which biases in our texts, going unrecognized, have been able to infiltrate our culture and so lend a measure of (alleged) legitimacy to such aspects of our history as anti-Semitism and the abuse of women.[3]

These, then, are appropriate places for the hermeneutic of suspicion.

Our forebears were clearly aware, however, that a hermeneutic of suspicion could be *mis*applied. "There's a double meaning here!" cries Shakespeare's Benedict excitedly when Beatrice comes to call him in to dinner: but the comedy of the situation depends on the fact that Benedict is quite wrong. There is no double meaning at all. Beatrice means just what she says. Hence this delightful scene may serve as a warning. Yes, we need to be alive to the need *at times* for suspicion, as when something jars us. But an unbridled habit of suspicion has its dangers, too. There is an interesting moment in one of George MacDonald's visionary novels, *Phantastes*, where the hero, traveling through fairyland, finds himself accompanied by a shadow. This shadow has a strange effect on what it touches.

> Once, as I passed by a cottage, there came out a lovely fairy child, with two wondrous toys, one in each hand. The one was the tube through which the fairy-gifted poet looks when he beholds the same thing everywhere; the other that through which he looks when he combines into new forms of loveliness those images of beauty which his own choice has gathered from all regions wherein he has traveled. Round the child's head was an aureole of emanating rays. As I looked at him in wonder and delight, round crept from behind me the something

dark, and the child stood in my shadow. Straightway he was a commonplace boy, with a rough, broad-brimmed straw hat, through which brim the sun shone from behind. The toys he carried were a multiplying glass and a kaleidoscope. I sighed and departed.[4]

As he journeys on, the traveler finds that the shadow is beginning to have an effect on him, which he finds "dreadful." It is this:

> I now began to feel something like satisfaction in the presence of the shadow. I began to be rather vain of my attendant, saying to myself, "In a land like this, with so many illusions everywhere, I need his aid to disenchant the things around me. He does away with all appearances, and shows me things in their true color and form. And I am not one to be fooled with the vanities of the common crowd. I will not see beauty where there is none. I will dare to behold things as they are. And if I live in a waste instead of in a paradise, I will live knowing where I live."[5]

The trouble is, of course—and as his journey continues the traveler realizes this—he has no way of knowing whether the shadow is actually showing him things as they are, or whether his more generous vision is doing that. And that is the problem with an uncontrolled hermeneutic of suspicion. No one wants to be a fool, taken in by everything. Some things have to be seen through. But as C. S. Lewis used to point out, "seeing through" things can be overdone. We "see through" things in order to "see" what is beyond them. If, however, we insist on seeing through *everything*, we shall in the end see nothing at all: "a wholly transparent world is an invisible world."[6] The path not merely to knowledge, but more importantly to wisdom, lies in schooling ourselves not only to see *through* things (occasionally necessary though that may be) but in general rather to *see* them.

The church chose the biblical texts—not quickly or without dispute, as the by-no-means pure and perfect history of the formation of the canon indicates[7]—because she believed that they witnessed to her faith, the faith she had received from the apostles, the faith that was enshrined in the Rule of Faith. It is in the light of their witness to that, and not of their witness to anything else—however odd or fascinating or even important—that they are finally to be judged. To put it another way, and in the current jargon, the "implied reader" of these texts is a believer, a member of the people of God. Those who count themselves in the fellowship of that people will therefore approach the biblical texts not with suspicion but in a spirit of hope and generosity—*fides quaerens intellectum*, faith seeking understanding—which surely implies at the very least a willingness to try to understand and interpret them in the light of what those who put them together as a collection thought they were saying. Bearing in mind Benedict's scene with Beatrice, one might also argue for that on the grounds of mere common sense. Sometimes a cigar is just a cigar. Sometimes there is no subtext. Sometimes, even if there is a subtext, it is not important. And even if there is a subtext and it is important, that does not let you off addressing the text. I often recall with pleasure the words of the classical scholar George Kennedy, speaking to a group of New Testament specialists: remember, he said, "ancient writers sometimes meant what they said and occasionally even knew what they were talking about."[8] I hope the New Testament specialists appreciated his gentle irony.

Two notes tend to characterize allegedly "objective" studies that give away too much to a hermeneutic of suspicion. One is the factoring in (generally without discussion or even acknowledgment of its presence) of a facile reductionism that simply rules as unhistorical any account of miracle—thereby importing into the inquiry a *philosophical* claim that has nothing to do with historical critical method as Schleiermacher proposed it, that is in itself highly debatable, and that, in the case of Jesus of Nazareth, is manifestly contradicted by every strand of tradition about him that we possess, including those hostile to him.[9] A classic example of this kind of prejudice was offered recently by Roy W. Hoover, a member of the Jesus Seminar. Commenting on a debate between the philosopher William Lane Craig and the New Testament scholar Gerd Lüdemann over the resurrection of Jesus,[10] Hoover made the preposterous claim (yet clearly he did not see it as preposterous) that because Craig, as a trained philosopher, was "open" to the possibility that there may be other levels and kinds of reality in the universe than those that can be perceived or investigated by scientific naturalism, he was thereby less "open" in his view of things, less committed to "truth," than was Lüdemann, who would not allow for *any* possibilities other than those comprehensible by scientific naturalism.[11] In other words, because Craig was *more* open, therefore he was *less* open. To which "hot ice and wondrous strange snow," what can one say?—save that it involves a commitment to dogmatic skepticism, a blind faith in positivist naturalism, that has taken leave of both logic and common sense. Hoover's extraordinary claim is based, so far as one can see, on little more than an observation (citing Gordon Kaufman) that "the idea of a divine super-Self *outside* of or beyond the universe...boggles the mind"[12]—an observation that Hoover appears to think constitutes an argument.[13] Of course, the observation in itself is correct, as the psalmist noted millennia ago (Ps. 139.6). The psalmist, however, was neither so foolish nor so arrogant as to think that because he could not conceive of something, therefore it could not or did not exist. Looked at from another angle, Hoover's comments are a classic example of what Walter Ong has identified as "the tendency of the past few centuries to overspatialize the universe so that everything is reduced to models picturable in space, and what is unpicturable ('unimagineable' is often the term invoked) is discarded as impossible or unreal."[14]

Such reductionism inevitably finds those who originally handed on the gospel tradition to have been either fools or falsifiers. And this is a second characteristic of many of these "objective" narratives: that the latest narrator is the one who at last understands Jesus and can tell the story as it should have been told, were it not for the guile or stupidity of those claimed first to have been eyewitnesses and ministers of the word. I would advise readers to prick up their ears and exercise their own hermeneutic of suspicion whenever they find a comment on the Scriptures something like the following:

> Jesus' followers did not grasp the subtleties of his position and reverted, once Jesus was not there to remind them, to the view they had learned from John the Baptist. As a consequence of this reversion, and in the aura of the emerging view of Jesus as a cult figure analogous to others in the Hellenistic mystery religions, the gospel writers overlaid the tradition of sayings and parables with their own 'memories' of Jesus. They constructed their memories out of the common lore, drawn in large part from the Greek Bible, the message of John the Baptist, and their own emerging convictions about Jesus as the expected

messiah—the Anointed. The Jesus of the gospels is an imaginative theological construct into which has been woven traces of that enigmatic sage from Nazareth—traces that cry out for recognition and liberation from the firm grip of those whose faith overpowered their memories.

When I first read that paragraph to a group of my students, they thought that I was joking—that I had made it up, and that it was a deliberate caricature. Their view was entirely understandable. It is probably difficult for anyone who is not a professional academic to imagine that such breath-taking arrogance could be intended seriously. Nonetheless, my students were wrong. I was not joking, I had not made it up, and it is not a caricature. It is a quotation from a real book, *The Five Gospels*, published in 1993 by members of the Jesus Seminar.[15] It is indeed fascinating that a group of self-designated "critical scholars," whose expressed criterion was "to make empirical, factual evidence—evidence open to confirmation by independent neutral observers—the controlling factor in historical judgments,"[16] should nonetheless have tolerated a hypothesis of their own that contradicts virtually all the evidence we have and for which in itself there is no evidence at all.

Yet the real problem with such a claim as is here made was essentially stated fifty or so years ago by C. S. Lewis. Lewis was familiar with the idea that the real behavior and purpose and teaching of Christ "came very rapidly to be misunderstood and misrepresented by his followers, and has been recovered or exhumed by modern scholars."[17] Having pointed to the same phenomenon in other fields of academic discourse, and the degree to which its suppositions in those fields were regularly discredited, he concluded: "The idea that any man or writer should be opaque to those who lived in the same culture, spoke the same language, shared the same habitual imagery and unconscious assumptions, and yet be transparent to those who have none of these advantages, is in my opinion preposterous. There is an *a priori* improbability in it which almost no argument and no evidence could counterbalance."[18] Exactly!

One of the most thought-provoking passages in Northrop Frye's *The Great Code* is where he says that biblical critics have generally been useless to him because they cast no light on how or why a poet might read the Bible.[19] Yet poets *do* read the Bible, and musicians and painters and sculptors, too. What is it that Dante and Handel and Botticelli and da Vinci have found there that biblical criticism misses? "Some dreams," said George MacDonald in his novel *Lilith*, "some poems, some musical phrases, some pictures, wake feelings such as one never had before, new in colour and form—spiritual sensations, as it were, hitherto unproved."[20] But how can that happen? Samuel Taylor Coleridge, in connection with the creation and enjoyment of poetry, spoke of "that willing suspension of disbelief for the moment, which constitutes poetic faith."[21] Coleridge was right. We shall find nothing of value in any text, including Holy Scripture, unless we try to listen to it on its own terms: and this, to be fair to Schleiermacher, was what he asked for. We must at some point abandon the hermeneutic of suspicion. And a problem with some historical critical studies, including some of the best known, is that they simply refuse to do this. Half a century ago, Lewis detected what he saw as a worrying tendency in some educators to encourage a thoughtless "debunking" of the values that earlier ages had held dear.[22]

Marilynne Robinson sees the phenomenon as by now in full and virulent bloom:

> There is an outpouring these days of scholarly looking books about the Bible. They might appear to depart from more traditional works on this venerable subject in their tone of condescension toward biblical texts and narratives, toward the culture that produced them, toward God... The intention behind these books seems to be only the one that is usual just now, to discredit in the course of laying blame. This is the purpose and method of much contemporary scholarship. Debunking exhausts its subjects, which must have some remnant of respectability about them to give meaning, or at least frisson, to the enterprise. And since the Bible does have a certain aura of sanctity about it yet, it offers the hope that there is discrediting still to be done, and this makes it an attractive subject.[23]

I hope that Robinson exaggerates: certainly there are exceptions, and there are many within the scholarly guild who protest against the tendencies she describes as heartily as she does. We have referred and will refer to a number of them in the course of this study. Still, Robinson does describe something that is really happening. I recently had to preach on Saint Mark's version of the Feeding of the Five Thousand and the Walking on the Water (Mark 6:34-52). By way of interest, I looked up what John Dominic Crossan had to say of these narratives in his *Historical Jesus*.[24] "For me," Crossan writes, "two different traditions, one of bread and fish, another of bread and wine, symbolically ritualized, after his death, the open commensality of Jesus' lifetime." What he finds "of present interest" in these stories is, however, "to watch how *general community, leadership group,* and *specific leader* intertwine."

> [T]he bread and fish Eucharist was originally a post-resurrectional confession of Jesus' continued presence at the meals of the believing community. Open commensality survived as ritualized meal. Once narrative gospels were composed that tradition was placed both before the resurrection, in the common source for Mark 6 and John 6, and after the resurrection, in Luke 24 and John 21. Even more fascinating, however, are those fleeting but tantalizing glimpses we catch across the bread and fish tradition as it moves from *general community* to *leadership group* and on to *specific leaders.*[25]

In sum, Crossan's thesis about all Jesus' "nature" miracles is that they "are actually credal statements about ecclesiastical authority."[26]

Opinions as to whether Crossan is right, either about church history or what lies behind the texts, will vary. Some of his views depend on narratives of interdependence and relationship between the canonical gospels and other texts (some of them hypothetical) that I have elsewhere characterized as "implausible."[27] Obviously, I have not here set out his arguments in full. But my purpose in this study is not to deal with the likelihood or unlikelihood of Crossan's proposals. I do not even wish to draw conclusions about them from the fact (of which he makes no secret) that his personal experience of Christianity has involved problems with "ecclesiastical authority."[28] My present point is simply this: whatever he is doing, and whether he is right or wrong, he is manifestly *not* carrying out Schleiermacher's hermeneutical project of discovering the author's intent. For while the evangelists may indeed have had some peripheral interest in issues of leadership, while they may even have had a marginal interest in the nature of the food that was consumed, these are hardly the salient features of their narrative. What *is* salient is the way in which they remember the man Jesus, which is, presumably, the way in which their communities remembered him: as one who fed his people when that seemed impossible, as one who came to his followers even when all seemed lost amid darkness and storm. What is also obvious is that the evangelists' and/or their communities found this memory important: the feeding is the only miracle that occurs in all four gospels; Matthew and Mark are so keen on it that they give us two versions; and the sequence feeding-walking on water occurs in both synoptic and Johannine traditions. In other words, it was something they *wanted* to remember. In the course of telling and retelling, one guesses that the memory has been touched by other images and reflections—Mosaic, Eucharistic. But the central narrative, the central memory, remains. Naturally, it is a memory of something extraordinary, in the most literal sense of that expression, and that, presumably, is one reason why they went on talking about it. But on any honest hearing, that *was* what they went on talking about, and so the Christian community has heard and understood them for two thousand or so years, in its art and in its teaching. Crossan, however, is not listening to their memory at all. He shows no interest in what they actually say. He is cross-examining them, as a lawyer cross-examines a witness who is known to be lying. And since false witness, hidden trails, and evasions are what he is looking for, it is hardly surprising that false witness, hidden trails, and evasions are what, if anything, he finds.

This is the hermeneutic of suspicion swollen to idolatry.

As coda to the foregoing, it may be useful to acknowledge briefly three figures from the nineteenth and early twentieth century: Karl Marx, Friedrich Nietzsche, and Sigmund Freud, in whose names, Julia Kristeva says, is subsumed the outbreak "of something quite new within Western society and discourse," of which the primary goal was "to reformulate an ethics."[29] There can be no doubt that Marx, Nietsche, and Freud have powerfully, if in general indirectly, exercised an influence in making "suspicion" almost normative in some circles with regard to religious texts, and, indeed, with regard to religion itself. Each saw religion as a cover for something else.

Marx saw religion as an opiate whereby the economically oppressed were consoled for injustice in the present by the prospect of happiness hereafter. By thus directing workers' attentions away from their present griefs, religion deadened their sense of misery, and so hindered them from trying to do anything about it. Hence, religion served to preserve the economic status quo.

Nietzsche saw religion as elevating weakness and a slave morality, and so giving comfort to slaves and misfits who were incapable of the master morality of the truly courageous and creative, among whom strength of will was an ultimate virtue.

Freud saw religion as a mode of replacing the (inevitably) failed father figures of our real lives with an illusory (in Freud's sense—that is, *wished for*, whether real or not) heavenly father figure who would not fail.

Of course, each of these critiques had in it an element of truth. Religious institutions *have* served to uphold oppressors; religion *is* at times a prop for failures and misfits;

religion *is* sometimes a matter of wish fulfillment. So much may be granted. Yet each critique also involved a logical fallacy, and in each case it was the same fallacy: namely, the notion that you can show an idea to be false by discrediting those who make use of it. You cannot. If you could, then of course the ideas of Marx, Nietzsche, and Freud would also have to be dismissed, since manifestly the proposals of all three have been asserted at times by fools and at times by charlatans.

Notes

1. Schleiermacher, *Hermeneutics*, 180.
2. Elisabeth Schüssler Fiorenza, *In Memory of Her: A Feminist Reconstruction of Christian Origins* (New York: Crossroad, 1984) 45.
3. I am grateful to my friend and colleague Cynthia Crysdale for heightening my attention to this in conversation. See also the enlightening remarks of André LaCocque, *The Captivity of Innocence: Babel and the Yahwist* (Eugene: Cascade, 2010) 131–33.
4. George MacDonald, *Phantastes*, ch. IX.
5. Ibid.
6. C. S. Lewis, *The Abolition of Man: Reflections on education with special reference to the teaching of English in the upper forms of schools* (Oxford: Oxford University, revised edition 1946 [1943]), 46–47.
7. Karl Barth, *Church Dogmatics* 1.1.§11.2.501–502; J. N. D. Kelly, *Early Christian Creeds* 242–54; Stephen E. Fowl, *Engaging Scripture: A Model for Theological Interpretation* (Oxford: Blackwell, 1998), 5–6.
8. George Kennedy, "Classical and Christian Source Criticism" in *The Relationships Among the Gospels: An Interdisciplinary Dialogue*. William O. Walker, Jr., ed. Trinity University Monograph Series in Religion 5. (San Antonio, Texas: Trinity University Press, 1978), 126.

9. See e.g., Craig S. Keener, *The Historical Jesus of the Gospels* (Grand Rapids, Mich.: Eerdmans, 2009) 241–42; Pagola, *Jesus*, 163–75; Meier, *Marginal Jew*, 2.617–772; E. P. Sanders, *Jesus and Judaism*, 157–73. Of course I do not cite these scholars (and the list could be lengthened almost indefinitely) as agreeing on the significance of Jesus' mighty acts, merely on the fact of them.

10. *Jesus' Resurrection Fact or Figment?: A Debate Between William Lane Craig and Gerd Lüdemann*, Paul Copan and Ronald K. Tacelli, eds. (Downers Grove, Ill.: InterVarsity Press, 2000).

11. op. cit. 127–29.

12. op. cit. 127, citing Gordon D. Kaufman, *In Face of Mystery: A Constructive Theology* (Cambridge: Harvard University Press, 1993) 305–306.

13. For Craig's devastating critique of Hoover, see *Jesus' Resurrection Fact or Figment?* 202–203.

14. Walter Ong, S. J., *The Presence of the Word: Some Prolegomena for Cultural and Religious History* (Yale: Yale University Press, 1967), 7. What Ong here critiques is, of course, precisely the position taken by Kaufman. Kaufman, following a recital of those "evils of modernity" for which Christianity "may be an important root," such as imperialism, racism, and sexism—apropos which one naturally wonders whether Kaufman *really* thinks these things began with Christianity or are uniquely to be associated with "modernity," and whether it is possible he has never heard of ancient Assyria, Persia, Athens, or Rome—following this dubiously grounded recital, he declares, "What we know (or think we know) about the world in which we live suggests a picture very different from the one conveyed in Christian tradition: indeed, it makes the traditional picture, I suggest, literally unthinkable by us, unintelligible (though of course we can still *assert* it)" (op. cit. 305). Leaving aside the stunning concession involved in that parenthetical "or think we know" (what a highway there opens for the deconstructionist!) or any critique one might offer of the meaningless "literally," it is plain that Kaufman here falls precisely into the error described by Ong: which is to claim that because we cannot "picture" something, therefore it must be discarded "as impossible or unreal."

15. *The Five Gospels*, R. W. Funk, R. W. Hoover, and the Jesus Seminar, eds. (New York: MacMillan, 1993), 4.
16. *The Five Gospels* 34.
17. Lewis, "Modern Theology and Biblical Criticism," 157.
18. "Modern Theology and Biblical Criticism," 158.
19. Frye, *Great Code*, xvii.
20. George Macdonald, *Lillith*, Chapter 3.
21. Samuel Taylor Coleridge, *Biographia Literaria* (1817) XIV.
22. Lewis, *Abolition of Man* 7–19; cf. *That Hideous Strength* passim; *Screwtape Letters* chs. i, xxv; *Great Divorce* 35–43.
23. Robinson, *When I Was a Child I Read Books*, 95; cf. *Absence of Mind*, 29.
24. Crossan, *Historical Jesus*, 407.
25. Crossan, *Historical Jesus*, 402.
26. Crossan, *Historical Jesus*, 404.
27. Christopher Bryan, *The Resurrection of the Messiah* (Oxford and New York: Oxford University Press, 2011), 205–206; cf. Bryan, *Render to Caesar*, 65–67.
28. "[T]he more profound conflict was…between my vow of obedience and scholarship. The truth may make you free, but it may also make a lot of other people extremely annoyed" (John Dominic Crossan, *A Long Way from Tipperary: A Memoir* [New York: HarperSanFrancisco, 2000], xiii). I find Crossan's writing in this memoir to be both refreshing and direct: I enjoyed it more than anything else of his that I have read.
29. Kristeva, *Desire in Language*, 23.

V

SO WHAT DO WE DO?

SUCH IS THE FAIRLY CHAOTIC situation. Such is the divorce between church and academy. What then? My intention in what follows is to consider what those who are called to academic biblical study, whether in seminary or university, as students or as teachers, should be attempting or looking for, if they wish to pursue these studies faithfully in service to the church. What, in the present age and the present situation, is the task of the biblical scholar within the church? How can biblical scholarship relate to the church's need to understand and interpret her foundation documents? What has such scholarship to do with the church's apostolate? Those are the questions that I wish to consider.

With matters such as these, however questionable may be the place where I end up, I like at least to start from something that seems relatively incontrovertible. So what would be a solid place from which to start in this case? At least, I suggest, we may say with certainty that the Bible is *a thing written*. It is *literature*. To be sure, much of it had oral beginnings, "sacred story" became "sacred text" as James Sanders puts it, [1] and sometimes we can imagine how that happened: Israel's stories being told and retold long before they were written down, Jesus teaching his disciples but writing nothing, Paul dictating his letters to a secretary—for the Letter to the Romans, we even know the secretary's name (see 16:22). For many centuries, moreover—even up to the Renaissance—the Bible was handed on in cultures that regarded language as primarily a thing spoken rather than written, and therefore was experienced for the most part not as words on a page but as speech (this is a matter to which we shall return). All that granted, the fact remains that the Bible *as a whole* at no time existed merely orally. The canon of Holy Scripture—whichever canon we choose, Anglican, Jewish, Orthodox, Protestant, or Roman Catholic—is and always has been what its names say that it is: *ta biblia*, the little books, *hai graphai*, the Scriptures, that is, the Writings, and hence *ho biblos*, the book. And if, as Israel and the church believe, God has chosen to be revealed through such a book, then God has chosen to be revealed through such a process as this—through human words that have in the course of time become literature.

That asserted, I must concede that there are some who have recently questioned it. Walter Ong, broadly following James Nohrnberg, says that Scripture is "hardly a member of the class 'literature' but presents a rival kind of organization" because "the Bible actually ends with an explicit cast into the future, the explicit opposite of 'ever after.'"[2] My immense respect for Ong's wisdom and scholarship leave me reluctant to question any assertion of his. Nonetheless, in this case I must do so on two grounds. First, I am not at all sure that I can grant the premise. While I concede that the Bible's concluding "cast into the future" is theologically very important—a point to which I shall return—that does not mean that there are no literary parallels to it. Second, even if I were to grant the premise, the word "literature," at least in the sense in which I use it (which is, I think, the most common sense) refers, as its etymology would suggest, to what is produced by system of letters, that is, to what is written, to *writings*.[3] That a particular piece of literature is in some way unique in its organization (or in any other way) by no means removes it from the general class. Actually, every piece of literature that is not exactly the same as some other piece of literature is in some way unique: that does not mean that it is not literature. *Pace* Nohrnberg and Ong, then, I continue to maintain that, however or in whatever respects the Bible is unique (and there are many respects in which it is so), the Bible is still literature.

What, then, are we supposed to do with literature? In my view, any critique or discussion of a written text that is not concerned with listening to it for what it is trying to say is beside the point. "Those who are not interested in an author's matter can have nothing of value to say about his style or construction."[4] I am not, therefore, saying that there is no place at all for study that may be somewhat tangential as regards the central purpose of the text in question—say, a study of Shakespeare's plays that concentrates on how they may indirectly reflect different stages of his life and be connected to his world and work, or looking at Jane Austen's novels to see what they imply about mealtimes and food in her society. Such studies may be pleasurable and interesting in themselves, and may even open up for us aspects of the work that illuminate it as a whole. I have, in fact, just described two real books—Jonathan Bate's biography of Shakespeare called *Soul of the Age*, and Maggie Black and Deirdre Le Faye's *Jane Austen Cookbook*—both riveting reading if you are a fan of Shakespeare or Austen. All that granted, I would insist that if one wants really to get to grips with Shakespeare's work, then at some point one has to take it for what it was and was clearly intended to be, poetry and drama. One must finally make the effort to treat his plays as plays, as texts whose home is in the theater and whose true life is in performance. Similarly, if one really wants to get to grips with Austen, one must be willing to read her novels as novels: which means opening oneself to entering the world of her characters, to living with Elizabeth Bennett and Emma Woodhouse as they experience their lives, growing and changing in that experience.

So, then, what of the Bible insofar as it is literature? Here, too, I take it, the serious scholar must be seeking at least as a first move, and granting all the uncertainties and difficulties in such an attempt that we have noted, to listen to its various voices as they intended to be heard. In other words, Schleiermacher's original project is valid so far as it goes, and we shall need to undertake it. And presumably, if we want to do that, we are going to have to listen to them individually. Paul is not the same as John, and neither of them is the same as Mark: yet someone thought all three—and of course all the others—were worth including in the New Testament. The same thing may be said of the various books of the Old Testament. Thus, we need to try to hear what each is saying. That is our first task.

At this point let me digress. I have just referred to "the Old Testament." I am aware that the phrase is problematic, and I use it uneasily. To some extent I agree with James Sanders's characterization of it as "inept."[5] Yet even Sanders continues to use it,[6] and the fact is, I find even more inept the various well-intended neologisms such as "Hebrew Bible" with which we try to replace it. The neologisms are in general both clumsy and inaccurate. In respect of our Jewish friends, I suspect such coinages are also patronizing, not to say a tad dishonest. I am, for better or worse, a Christian interpreter of these texts, and therefore, in point of fact, they *do* stand for me as "old" in relation to "new": "old" not in the sense of being "superseded," "out of date," or "no longer relevant" (which view would make me, in fact, not an orthodox Christian at all but a Marcionite heretic), but "old" in the sense that, unlike

the New Testament, they were there from the very beginnings of Christianity, and because Jesus himself, not to mention his followers, interpreted his mission in terms of their
teaching and promises. I believe we best keep faith with our
Jewish bothers and sisters by being honest about our beliefs
and about what we are doing; and I am strengthened in this
conviction by finding it shared by no less doughty a foe of
supersessionism than Walter Brueggemann. As Christians,
Brueggemann writes, our study of the Scriptures of Israel
obliges us to explore "what happens when the text is brought
to our faith in Jesus of Nazareth as the Christ."[7]

To return to my main theme: we have described our first
task as that of listening to the individual voices that speak
to us in the Bible. But there is something else, for we have
also spoken of "the Bible"—the voices assembled as a whole.
What, then, of the Bible's "matter" when its voices are considered *together*? Indeed, we may well wonder whether such an
array of texts in two (actually, three) languages, ranging over
centuries in its production, deriving from vastly differing
cultures and sources, involving many genres, and represent-
ing vastly different interests, hopes, and experiences—we
may well wonder whether such an array can be said to have
a shared "matter" at all. Is there really a common concern?
A theme? And if so, what is it?

To put it another way, we are bound to ask how the Bible
that we have, even the various canons of different groups,
emerged in the form that we have. Northrop Frye was quite
right: "The Bible does not, for all its miscellaneous content,
present the appearance of having come into existence through
an improbable series of accidents; and, while it is certainly
the end product of a long and complex editorial process, the
end product needs to be examined in its own right."[8] Clearly,

if we claim to be studying, not merely "Jeremiah" or "John" but "the Bible," this, too, is an issue that we must explore. Here, then, is a second task.

But there is also surely a third: if there is in this body of material a "matter," a shared concern, what does that "matter" have to do with us? Why are we paying attention to the Bible at all? I think I know why I read Lindsey Davis's Falco books or have just watched *Tea with Mussolini.* So why do I read the Bible? What has been its significance throughout the two thousand or so years of its existence? What and how has it fed into people's lives and into the life of the church? What, if anything, and how, if at all, does it continue to do that?

So there emerge three tasks for the interpreter of Scripture:

> to listen so far as possible to the *individual* voices of Scripture and try to understand them;
> to consider the individual voices in relation to the *whole of Scripture,* asking how far an overall witness, a consensus, arises from Scripture, and if so what it is;
> and finally to ask how all that relates to the continuing life and witness of the Church up to and including our own day.

Let me concede at once that in practice, and even in principle, I doubt the three tasks are ever completely separable. As the poststructuralists and others remind us, in the most basic imaginable act of reading or listening, we bring to what we read a web of associations and memories, some of them literary (in the case of a biblical passage including but hardly limited to the rest of Scripture), some of them cultural, some social, some personal, and so on. There is no way of avoiding this. It is simply a part of reading and being human. When encountering the Scriptures—indeed when encountering any text or any art form—I naturally move in and out of contemplation or enjoyment of the thing before me, of other texts or art forms that are for me associated with it, and of my experience of life itself. My thoughts and understanding of the work before me, my response to it, will be a mosaic of all these things. Still, and all that granted, I believe that there is something useful to be obtained, if only by way of focusing our thoughts, in looking at each in turn of the three tasks—the three aspects of one task, if we will—that are involved for us in engaging the Bible's "matter." That is what I now propose to do.[9]

Notes

1. James A. Sanders, *From Sacred Story to Sacred Text: Canon as Paradigm* (Philadephia: Fortress, 1987).
2. See Ong, *Interfaces of the Word: Studies in the Evolution of Consciousness and Culture* (Ithaca and London: Cornell University, 1977); 261–62); Nohrnberg, "On Literature and the Bible," *Centrum* 2.2 (1974) 25–27.
3. *OED2*, "literature" 2, 3a, b, 4, 5; cf. *OLD*, "litteratura," 1, 2, 3.
4. C.. S. Lewis, letter to George Watson, October 9, 1962; in *Collected Letters* 3.1375; cf. John P. Meier, *A Marginal Jew* 1.11–12; Richard Bauckham, *Women in the Gospels: Studies of the Named Women in the Gospels* (Grand Rapids, Mich.: Eerdmans, 2002) xv.
5. Sanders, *Sacred Story to Sacred Text*, 3.
6. E.g., Sanders, *Sacred Story to Sacred Text*, 22–23 and passim.
7. See Walter Brueggemann, *Genesis* (Atlanta: John Knox Press, 1982), 7; see also his *Theology of the Old Testament: Testimony, Dispute, Advocacy* (Minneapolis: Fortress, 1997), 1, n.1.
8. *The Great Code*, xvii.

9. Although I do not use the word "intertextuality" in my main text, I think that what I have written there agrees more or less with the thought of poststructuralist Julia Kristeva when she coined the word "intertextualité" in the eighties of the last century. For Kristeva, if I understand her correctly, "intertextualité" (*pace* much subsequent use and misuse of the word on both sides of the Atlantic) was nothing to do with the influence of one writer on another, or with the sources of a written work, but with the fact that when one reads, meaning is not transferred directly from writer to reader, but is rather mediated or filtered by way of systems of signs that have been imparted to both writer and reader by other texts and signifying systems in the surrounding culture. Within a particular culture, texts are read, consciously or unconsciously, in the light of each other, and in this way intersect, absorbing and transforming each other so as to form a mosaic. "Intertextualité" is the transposition of systems of signs into other systems, leading naturally to new articulations of their enunciative and denotive position (see Julia Kristeva, *La Révolution du langage poétique* (Paris: Seuil, 1974), 59–60; cf. *Desire in Language: A Semiotic Approach to Literature and Art* [New York: Columbia University Press, 1980], 15, 65–66). As I consider Kristeva's reflections, I am further reminded of that extraordinary passage in which Marcel Proust describes a childhood experience of reading: see, *À la recherche du temps perdu, 1, Du coté de chez Swann* (Paris: Gallimard, 1913), 122–32.

▼

VI

THE FIRST TASK: LISTENING TO

THE INDIVIDUAL VOICES

IT WAS BENJAMIN JOWETT'S FIRST principle, "that Scripture has but one meaning—the meaning which it had to the mind of the Prophet or Evangelist who first uttered or wrote, to the hearers or readers who first received it."[1] There are elements in that assertion that are mistaken—we shall return to them—but there is also an element that proves valid, and lasting in its value, for it reflects one of the most important gifts that we inherit from the Enlightenment, which is the development of the historical-critical sense: that is, our awareness that the ancients were not simply the same as we are, and that we will understand them better if we try to hear them in the context of their own times and assumptions, which were not always the same as ours.

I say, "not always," for this is not to say that everything in a text from another generation must be alien to us. When we watch a play by an Attic dramatist or read Virgil's *Aeneid*, there are universal human values in them that come across almost whatever our level of information about their origins: this is a subject to which we shall need to return. For the moment, suffice it to say that historical critical sense reminds us that, even though we may have some things in common with Aeschylus or Virgil, still, the more we know about life and language in ancient Greece or Augustan Rome, the more closely we shall encounter them, and the closer we shall come to meeting them as they would, perhaps, have wished to be met.

The same is true of the Scriptures. On the one hand, a story such as the Parable of the Good Samaritan has an appeal that has led countless men and women over centuries to act more compassionately than they would otherwise have done, even though they had virtually no knowledge at all of the society or *mores* that the parable reflects. On the other hand, how much closer we come to these texts if we learn more about those other things!

Thus, all the disciplines that seminarians and theological students normally encounter in their survey biblical courses have their place. We will look for as much understanding as possible of biblical Hebrew, Aramaic, and the *koinē* or common Greek of the first Christian century. We will make use of all that can be learned of the form and wording of the texts by way of textual criticism, since it will be good to know, so far as possible, when we are encountering them in the forms in which their authors intended them to be heard, and when we are encountering them in forms reflecting the concerns— or even the mere copiers' errors—of those who passed them on. We shall be attentive to all the varied questions that may be asked by such inquirers as the historian, the sociologist, and the archeologist, since each may teach us something of how our texts were to be heard. We shall pay attention to the insights of rhetorical criticism, since these texts were certainly designed in the first instance to be heard, not looked at. We shall consider the various types of literary criticism: in particular, questions as to the texts' genre (what *kinds* of text are these?) and—since genre is a tool of meaning—what does that say about how they are to be understood? All these questions have their place, and each of these disciplines, if honestly pursued, can have something to teach us. The two latter—consideration of the texts as rhetoric, and consideration of genre—involve particular issues to which we shall need to return.

This plethora of possible questions and approaches means, among other things, that we may learn valuable things about our texts from those who do not necessarily share our views or our faith, as well as from those who do. It is a grave mistake in our reading to confine ourselves to the work of people with whom we agree, or to members of our own denomination, or even to Christians. The church cannot copyright her foundation documents, or say who may study them, and I do not think that it would be a good thing if she could. Free inquiry is another gift of the Enlightenment, and it is a fine gift. Anyone may study anything and from any point of view. Of course, and by the same token, we do not have to accept all of anyone's views or opinions about anything, but the thoughts of anyone who is pursuing honest questions with honest intent can inform us. While I am critical of various approaches to the Bible, such as those of the Jesus Seminar, I hope I will never be so ungenerous as to deny that I have learned from them—at the very least, because my disagreements have compelled me to ask myself why I disagree, and so to reflect more carefully on my own positions and assumptions. And of course it is not always a matter of learning from disagreements. Sometimes it is a matter of learning from those with whom we disagree precisely *because* they approach with a different outlook or with different questions. In particular, I am aware how much I have learnt from my Jewish friends as fellow students of these texts, and I confess my indebtedness over the years to such magnificent interpreters as Erich Auerbach, Daniel Boyarin, David Daube, Jon D. Levenson, Amy Jill Levine, Samuel Sandmel, and Geza Vermes.

One curious aspect of the present state of affairs is that I occasionally hear of students being warned against reading a particular scholar *because* that scholar is a Christian—Luke Timothy Johnson and N. T. Wright have both, in my hearing, come in for this kind of criticism. "You cannot trust their work," goes the argument, "because they are not objective: they go to the text determined to find support for the beliefs they already hold." Both these scholars, as it happens, hold particular views with which I disagree. That, however, is beside the point. The point is, according to the warning, I am to dismiss their discussions of, say, Saint Paul, not because on this or that issue I disagree with them, but simply on the ground *that they share some of Saint Paul's convictions.* This, apparently, is a *dis*qualification for commenting upon him! It places them, I suppose, among those whom the Jesus Seminar describes as "held captive by prior theological commitment."[2] Being captive in this way, they cannot be "truly academic," or "real historians."

The basis of the error here—and it is error, plain and simple, let us make no doubt of it—is the supposition that only "objective" or "presupposition-less" approaches can teach us anything. Thus, lovers can teach us nothing of love. The only persons who can teach us about love are those who look at the phenomenon "objectively" from outside. Dog and cat lovers can teach us nothing of dogs and cats. Only those who regard them as objects for the laboratory or the dissecting table can inform us. Leaving aside the fact that it is (as we have already noticed) impossible for any human being to approach anything without presuppositions, there is in any case no logical basis for supposing that knowledge of anything gained by external study of it is necessarily more valuable or in any sense more "true" than knowledge gained by experiencing it. Do we learn more of rain by reading books about rainfall and its effects, or by standing in the rain and feeling it in our hair and on our skin? Properly speaking, the answer is "neither": but we gain different *kinds* of knowledge, whose relative value depends on what we want or what we are trying to achieve.[3]

So far as the Bible, or any other text, is concerned, I would advise my students not to fear anyone who approaches the matter from *any* clearly described and openly expressed position. We can watch what they do, and if we think their presuppositions are affecting their judgment adversely, we can discount it. The ones to fear are those who are self-deceived or deceiving enough to claim that they approach their subject *without* presuppositions, for their entire work is based on an illusion.

The careful reader may have noticed that in setting the agenda for this chapter, I spoke of listening to the different *voices* of Scripture. I did not speak of *authors* or *authorship*. That is not because I regard authorial intent as irrelevant to meaning, as some suggest. But I do grant that the issue is problematic. Jowett, as we have seen, denied the possibility of *any* meaning for biblical texts apart from that intended by their authors: there can be, he declared, only "the meaning which it had to the mind of the Prophet or Evangelist who first uttered or wrote, to the hearers or readers who first received it." Yet the very form in which he stated that claim gives a hint of its problems. He used two phrases in apposition—but apposition indicates, or ought to indicate, that the expressions so placed refer to the same person or thing, or at least that one qualifies the other ("Wendy, my wife"). In the case at issue, however, how could Jowett possibly know that the "meanings" intended by prophets and evangelists and the "meanings" understood by those who heard them were always the same? From the way in which Paul finds himself arguing with his converts, it is perfectly clear that sometimes they were not (2 Cor 5:9-11; cf. 2 Peter 3:16).

To be fair to Jowett, it must be said that philosophical reflection over the last century or so has put us in a better position to understand this than was he: for if there is one thing that we should have learnt from the deconstructionists, it is surely that *words do not in fact have a single meaning, still less that their meaning is limited to authorial intent.* Indeed, we imply it ourselves every time we say something like, "Let's admit they wrote better than they knew," or even (as a friend of mine said recently), "I simply asked her to pass the marmalade and she burst into tears!"

It is not, of course, that texts can mean anything: that is how deconstructionism is sometimes portrayed, and it is nonsense. Whatever meaning we attribute to a text, we must be able to point to a rationale for it within the text itself, and there is such a thing as interpreting a text against itself—as, for example, when a recent London production of *Hamlet* set the play in a psychiatric hospital,[4] or a production of Mozart's *Don Giovanni* a few years back showed Don Giovanni at the end (as we say) "getting away with it," still up to his old tricks and enjoying himself in Hell.[5] Of course, there is a sense in which the Danish court in Shakespeare's play is something of a mental institution: but to make it *actually* a mental institution is to lose precisely the play's irony about politics and power struggles among those who are generally regarded as sane. [6] As for the trick with the end of *Don Giovanni*, that was to make a mockery of Mozart's music, Da Ponte's libretto, and the performances of a number of fine artists who evidently understood and honored exactly what *Don Giovanni* is about.

No, we should not interpret a text against itself. Nor is it true, though some would wish to make it so, that authorial intent is simply irrelevant to what a text means. If it were, why would we invite living authors to discuss their books? Why would those who believe that authorial intent is irrelevant to the meaning of a text bother to write books on the subject? Why, indeed, would one want to write or say anything at all? What would be the point? Authorial intent is not the only element in what a text means, but it is certainly *an* element, and if we try to ignore it completely we tie ourselves in knots.[7] When we deny our sense of a personality behind some of the texts of the New Testament we do a disservice to ourselves, to those who composed them, and to the texts themselves, failing to acknowledge that in encountering them we are also in some sense encountering a person.

Yet when all this has been considered, we have not yet come to the question of final importance. "Those who are not interested in an author's matter can have nothing of value to say about his style or construction." What, then, must we say of the "matter" of our biblical texts? Generally directly, occasionally indirectly, their central matter is always the same: it is God. I read recently of a university where the courses on the Old Testament were in two parts. First the students received "An Introduction to the History and Literature of the Hebrew Bible." Then, in the following semester, they could if they wished take an *optional* course on, "The Theology of the Hebrew Bible." Now, I dare say those who teach those courses do better than is claimed for them. I make no comment on what they actually teach since I do not know what it is. But someone needs to tell whoever designed the schedule that the sequence of events implied in the course titles, and still more the significance implied for them, is nonsense: and the same would be true of a similar approach to the New Testament. Those who told the biblical stories and those who wrote them down thought they were talking about things that had happened in history, no doubt, and surely thought they were creating literature of a sort. But they also thought they were talking and writing about God, and until we have engaged them on that subject, until we have listened to what they have to say and considered what may be our response to it, until we have engaged their *matter*, then we have not in any realistic sense had an "introduction" to their texts at all. We have stared at them from across the room, perhaps admired their exotic dress, wondered at their language, or listened to some tales about where they came from or how they got here. But we haven't been *introduced* to them, we haven't actually *met* them, and we certainly don't *know* them. Theology was not, for this literature, an afterthought. And it certainly was not optional.

In insisting on this concern, I do not regard myself as backing away from my earlier insistence that all who come with honest questions and convictions to the texts have something to contribute to the discussion. But I am insisting that while in this age our conversation, even within the fellowship of faith, must and should involve listening to many voices with many points of view, still, such conversation will be truly serious, even in terms of the purely academic, only when we do *not* cordon ourselves off from talking about *what the texts themselves are talking about.*

Notes

1. Jowett, "Interpretation," 378.
2. *The Five Gospels*, 5.
3. Cf. C. S. Lewis, "Meditation in a Toolshed," in *God in the Dock: Essays on Theology and Ethics*, Walter Hooper, ed. (Grand Rapids, Mich.: Eerdmans, 1970) 212–15.
4. *Hamlet*, directed by Ian Rickson, with Martin Sheen as Hamlet: the Young Vic, London, 2012. Charles Spencer wrote in a meticulously argued review: "I have seen duller and worse acted Hamlets, but none in which a director seemed so implacably and egotistically intent on twisting the play to his own dubious ends."
5. *Don Giovanni*, directed by Jugen Flimm, with Cecilia Bartoli as Donna Elvira and Rodney Gilfry as Don Giovanni: Zurich Opera, 2002 (available on DVD: ASIN: B00008G6EZ).
6. See James Schapiro, *A Year in the Life of William Shakespeare: 1599* (London: Faber and Faber / New York: Harper Collins, 2005), 282–83.
7. See Seàn Burke, *The Death and Return of the Author* (Edinburgh: Edinburgh University, 1992), especially 20–153; also David Brown, *Tradition and Imagination: Revelation and Change* (Oxford: Oxford University Press, 1999), 42–43.

VII

A DIGRESSION: "GREAT
LITERATURE?"

IN CONNECTION WITH REFLECTION ON the individual voices and texts of the Bible, it is perhaps appropriate to touch briefly on a question about them that I am asked from time to time on the basis of my background and primary training as *literary* critic. It is this: "What do I think of them *as literature*? Are they *great* literature?" Naturally, I hedge! "It all depends on what you mean by 'great,'" I say, or even, "It depends whom you ask!" Some critics—including many in antiquity—would see greatness as linked to certain canons of style and language. And, notoriously, by canons of style that were prominent during the early Christian centuries, the books of the New Testament do not fare well. They were regarded with scorn by cultured despisers of Christianity such as Celsius, just because they were not polished in these respects, and among the cultured even those who defended the New Testament did so not along lines of challenging these standards or their relevance, but rather by conceding them, and saying that the fact that God consented to use such feeble instruments as these was a sign of God's gracious willingness to be revealed to the simplest and humblest. In other words, the very weakness of the text revealed *condescensio Dei*, God's condescension: God's willingness to be amongst us whatever the cost. That defense is by no means without force in respect to certain questions, notably the issue of errors in Scripture over matters of scientific or historical fact.[1] With respect to the *literary* quality of these texts, however—their greatness or otherwise—I would say that it rather misses the point, for the use of such criteria to decide issues of this kind is in itself quite unsatisfactory.

What, after all, does one mean by calling a text "great"? In the 1950s, when my primary field of study was literature and especially English literature, I was brought to think— and I still think—that the greatest works of art (not only in literature, but also in the performative and plastic arts) are those *that continue to sustain and reward the most considered and careful attention by the largest number and variety of people over the longest period of time.* [2] As George Steiner points out, "No stupid literature, art or music lasts."[3] So then, one does not discover whether a work is great by setting up or discerning rules and then deciding whether or not it keeps them. One discovers that, at least for oneself, by giving to the work one's fullest attention, so far as one can on its own terms—by surrendering to it, if you will—and then seeing how it rewards such attention. In other words, Glory Boughton was in the right of it: "Why do we have to read poetry? Why 'Il Penseroso'? Read it and you'll know why. If you still don't know, read it again. And again."[4]

By that standard there can then be no doubt: the biblical texts are great texts. At the precise moment when the author or authors of Genesis ceased to write, or Paul stopped dictating Romans, I dare say the status of what they had written, its greatness or otherwise, was open to debate. It is so no longer. If you do not experience their greatness, then at least be humble—which essentially means, be realistic: admit your own inadequacy. It is absurd to deny or even question the greatness of texts that, as we have already noticed, have over two thousand years rewarded the profound attention of millions and millions of by no means trivial people in ways that have enabled them to live lives of meaning and grace. *Securus iudicat orbis terrarum.*

There is, however, another approach to this kind of question that may be more profitable than asking whether our texts meet some arbitrarily imposed standard of greatness such as Attic Greek. Given that certain works *do* powerfully affect us, and *have* powerfully affected millions over long periods of time, we may reasonably ask *why* that is so. This is not a matter of looking for rules, but of asking what it is about some pieces of literature that causes them to work on us in certain ways. In a literature as varied as the Bible, there will be, of course, many particular things to be said of particular books, and for consideration of those one will naturally turn to commentaries on the individual books. Erich Auerbach in his book *Mimesis*—arguably the most important single work of literary criticism written in the twentieth century—did, however, point to two characteristics in particular that mark much of the biblical literature.[5]

The first is that biblical narrative is characterized by the externalization of only so much of the phenomena as is necessary for the purpose of telling the story. In a narrative such as that of the binding of Isaac, and in marked contrast to Homeric narrative, when the characters speak,

> their speech does not serve, as does speech in Homer, to manifest, to externalize thoughts—on the contrary, it serves to indicate thoughts which remain unexpressed. God gives his command in direct discourse, but he leaves his motives and his purpose unexpressed; Abraham, having received the command, says nothing and does what he has been told to do. The conversation between Abraham and Isaac on the way to the place of sacrifice is only an interruption of the heavy silence and makes it all the more burdensome. The two of

them, Isaac carrying the wood and Abraham with fire and knife, "went together." Hesitantly, Isaac ventures to ask about the ram, and Abraham gives the well-known answer. Then the text repeats: "So they went both of them together." Everything remains unexpressed. The biblical text is characterized by the externalization of only so much of the phenomena as is necessary for the purpose of narrative, all else left in obscurity; the decisive points of the narrative alone are emphasized, what lies between is non-existent, time and place are undefined and call for interpretation; thoughts and feelings remain unexpressed, are only suggested by the fragmentary speech; the whole, permeated with the most unrelieved suspense and directed toward a single goal...remains mysterious and 'fraught with background.'...God is always so presented in the Bible, for he is not comprehensible in his presence, as is Zeus; it is always only 'something' of him that appears, he always extends into the depths.[6]

This, I believe, is true of much of the narrative in both Old and New Testaments, and is one source of its power to stimulate our imaginations: there is always more to reflect on, more to imagine.

A second characteristic is particularly noted by Auerbach in reference to the New Testament. Here is an extract from his comments on the narrative of Peter's denial in the gospels. He contrasts it with Petronius's wonderfully gossipy dinner guest describing Trimalchio's wife Fortunata (*Satyricon* 37-38), and Tacitus's account of Pannonius's rebellion (*Annals* 1.66).

Peter, whose personal account may be assumed to be the basis of the story, was a fisherman from Galilee, of humblest background and humblest education. The other participants in the night scene in the court of the High Priest's palace are servant

girls and soldiers.... A tragic figure from such a background, a
hero of such weakness, who yet derives the highest force from
his very weakness...is incompatible with the sublime style of
classical antique literature. But the nature and the scene of the
conflict also fall entirely outside the domain of classical antiquity. Viewed superficially, the thing is a police action and its
consequences; it takes place entirely among everyday men and
women of the common people; anything of the sort could be
thought of in antique terms only as farce or comedy. Yet why
is it neither of these? Why does it arouse in us the most serious and significant sympathy? Because it portrays something
which neither the poets nor the historians of antiquity ever set
out to portray: the birth of a spiritual movement in the depths
of the common people, from within the everyday occurrences
of common life, which thus assumes an importance it could
never have assumed in antique literature. What we witness is
the awakening of 'a new heart and a new spirit.' All this applies
not only to Peter's denial but also to every other occurrence
related in the New Testament.[7]

This is a remarkable observation that, while it speaks directly
to the question of this literature's "greatness," also speaks to
one of the New Testament's central theological claims: that
in Christ, "There is no longer Jew or Greek, there is no longer slave or free, there is no longer male and female; for all
of you are one in Christ Jesus" (Gal. 3:28; cf. Col. 3:11). Yet
Auerbach was not by profession a biblical scholar—still less
a New Testament scholar. He was not concerned to make
theological points. He was a German philologist and com-
parative literary critic, and his concern was to examine "the
Representation of Reality in Western Literature."[8] He was,
incidentally (but surely not "incidentally" from his point
of view) also a Jew who under Hitler's regime had received

appalling treatment from Nazis. Such a personal history might well have led him to despise any Christian text. It did not, however, because his literary judgment guided him in the consideration of texts and arose out of a profound and sustained willingness to begin by paying attention to what they said and what they were.

One notes, by the way, that Auerbach was also not especially interested in historical questions. He does not discuss the historicity of Homer, or Genesis, or Petronius, and scarcely touches even on that of Tacitus. Yet when the question of historicity forces itself on his attention from the very nature of the text, what he says—in passing—is striking: Peter's "personal account may be assumed to be the basis of the story." We are a million miles from John Dominic Crossan's (repeated) assertion, "I take it for granted that early Christianity knew nothing about the passion beyond the fact itself."[9] In Crossan's discussion of the passion narratives, he has nothing to say about Peter's denial. The passages in the (all four) canonical gospels where it is described do not even appear in the "Text Index" of Crossan's *Historical Jesus*. Perhaps this was inevitable: the story of Peter's denial, as Auerbach's reaction to it shows, by its very nature cuts clean across Crossan's assertion that the Markan passion narrative as a whole "is magnificent theological fiction"—and I note that Crossan cannot give even that modest praise without a scratch: "but entailing a dreadful price for Judaism."[10] This is nonsense, of course. Not Mark's narrative, but the *misuse* of Mark's narrative, entailed that "dreadful price." Yet although this is not in itself a trivial matter, the real and fundamental difference between Auerbach and Crossan is that Auerbach had a broad, profound, and genial understanding of literature in general that enabled him to distinguish fictions from reminiscence; and he had that because *he habitually paid attention to what a text actually said.* Crossan, by contrast, does not.

Auerbach treated the Bible exactly as he treated any other book, and his knowledge of other books enabled him to see that it was indeed unique—"not like any other book"— and certainly not like any book that had been written before it. Remember, again, he spoke neither as a New Testament scholar nor even as a Christian, but simply as a philologist and a literary critic, when he said:

> A scene like Peter's denial fits into no antique genre. It is too serious for comedy, too contemporary and everyday for tragedy, politically too insignificant for history—and the form which it was given is one of such immediacy that its like does not exist in the literature of antiquity. This may be judged by a symptom which at first glance may seem insignificant: the use of direct discourse. The maid says, "And you also were with Jesus of Nazareth!" He answers: "I don't know, and I don't understand what you're saying." Then the maid says to the bystanders: "This is one of them." And when Peter repeats his denial, the bystanders speak up: "Surely you're one of them, for you're a Galilean by your speech." I do not believe that there is a single passage in an antique historian where direct discourse is employed in this fashion in a brief, direct dialogue.[11]

One could happily quote more, for Auerbach's entire discussion and analysis is fascinating, but I think I have done what I wanted to do—which was not to present Auerbach's views (a thing unnecessary, since Auerbach can speak very well for himself: I commend my readers to him, and especially to chapters 1 and 2 of *Mimesis*), but rather to show why the biblical literature, including the literature of the New Testament, deserves to be called "great," and also why not dissection, not problematizing, but attention, is the way to perceive that greatness. If we are not listening, we have no reason to be surprised if we do not hear anything.

We are talking about what might, I suppose, be called "proper respect." In the Oxford English School, I learned an important principle from J. R. R. Tolkien, lecturing to us on *Gawain and the Green Knight*: namely, that when we were studying any text that had stood the test of time—which is virtually to say, any great text—what we were studying was almost certainly greater than anything any of us might have to say about it. If that was true of *Gawain* (and it was), it is certainly true of Holy Scripture. The history of biblical criticism (as of literary criticism generally) is littered with the wreckage of those who thought they sat in judgment on the text. In reality, it is generally the text that sits in judgment on us.

Notes

1. Christopher Bryan, *And God Spoke: The Authority of the Bible for the Church Today* (Cambridge, Mass.: Cowley, 2002), 48–49, 67–69.
2. For the approach I describe, see C. S. Lewis's seminal *An Experiment in Criticism* (Cambridge: Cambridge University Press, 1961).
3. George Steiner, *Real Presences* (London: Faber and Faber, 1989), 11.
4. Marilynne Robinson, *Home* (New York: Farrar, Straus, and Giroux, 2008), 21.
5. Erich Auerbach, *Mimesis: The Representation of Reality in Western Literature*, Willard R. Trask, trans. (Princeton: Princeton University, 1953 [1946]).
6. Auerbach, *Mimesis* 11–12.
7. Auerbach, *Mimesis* 42–43.

8. This is the subtitle to *Mimesis* (see above, n. 5).
9. John Dominic Crossan, *The Historical Jesus: The Life of a Mediterranean Jewish Peasant* (HarperSanFrancisco, 1991), 387; cf. 375, 390; cf. Crossan, *The Cross that Spoke: The Origins of the Passion Narrative* (San Francisco: Harper and Row, 1988) 405.
10. Crossan, *Historical Jesus*, 390.
11. Auerbach, *Mimesis* 46. In this passage I have slightly altered Trask's translation of the German.

VIII

THE SECOND TASK: RELATING THE PARTS TO THE WHOLE

(1) THE RULE OF FAITH AND THE QUESTION OF HISTORY.

The second task of the biblical scholar is, I have said, to consider the individual voices in relation to the *whole of Scripture*; to reflect how far an overall witness, a consensus, arises from Scripture, and if so, what it is.

Our forebears, over centuries and after numerous disputes and revisions, gradually recognized as sacred Scripture the various collections of texts (or "canons") that constitute our Bibles. Obviously, those who did this thought that those texts related to each other, and in a positive way, as having a shared "matter," a common theme. So, of course, did those who originally wrote them, or at least the later ones. When Mark says that the gospel of Jesus begins "as it is written," when Matthew begins his gospel with a genealogy of figures from the Old Testament, when Paul speaks of Jesus as "of the seed of David" (Mark 1:2, Matt 1:1-17, Rom 1:3), they are assuming such a common theme. And so, I suggest, may we, without a great effort of imagination.

To begin with, as Northrop Frye points out, speaking purely from a literary point of view, the Bible does have "a beginning, and an end, and some traces of a total structure. It begins where time begins, with the creation of the world; it ends where time ends, with the Apocalypse, and it surveys human history in between, or the aspect of history it is interested in, under the symbolic names of Adam and Israel."[1]

That is true, so far as it goes. But we may go further. We may note that the aspect of human history the Bible is interested in does not, in fact, center upon humanity at all, but upon God: the God of creation, the God of Israel, the God of the Christian Church. When God's breath moves over the face of the waters, when the LORD asks Abram, "Where is your wife Sarah?," when Jesus dies upon the cross drawing forth the centurion's confession, or else, risen, is known to his disciples in the breaking of bread, then, if we are trying to listen to this literature for what it tells us—for its "matter"—then we must understand that in its universe, the universe of these particular texts, we are hearing of the divine presence, being ourselves but dust, albeit beloved dust.[2] Evelyn Underhill reminded an Archbishop of Canterbury on the eve of a Lambeth Conference that the most interesting thing about religion is God. By the same token, we need to remember that God is also the most interesting thing about the Bible.

Our forebears believed, moreover, that the biblical narrative spoke of God in a special way. They saw it as witnessing to God's continuing work and grace in the world and among God's people: a story of creation and fall, of the call of Abraham, of Exodus, Sinai, settlement, exile, and return; and among Christians, a subsequent story of the life, death, and resurrection of Jesus Christ for us and for our salvation, of the gift of the Holy Spirit and the foundation of the church, and of the still future, final presence of Christ as savior and judge of the world. It is a story that was from the early days of Christianity characterized as the Canon (that is, "standard") of Faith (κανών πίστεως) or the Rule of Faith (regula fidei).

It is a story that to this day is confessed by much of the universal church in those finally evolved and defined versions of the Canon or Rule of Faith that we now know as the Nicene (Niceno-Constantinopolitan, to be precise) and Apostles' Creeds.

Insofar as our biblical canon as a whole has a "matter," this creedal story, this Rule of Faith, is it. Every single text of Scripture relates in some way or other to some part of it. In particular, texts of the New Testament relate to one group of events in that story above all others, namely, the passion and resurrection of Jesus Christ: that Jesus was crucified under Pontius Pilate and God raised him from the dead. The basic affirmation of 1 Corinthians 15, "Christ died...he was buried...he has been raised...he was seen" is reflected in each gospel's passion and resurrection narrative, which is not to say that the one is a literary or scribal development of the other, but rather that the two, the narrative and the summary—in essence, the gospel and the creed—stand together from the beginning, inseparable.[3]

Thus, the task of biblical scholarship as understood by Jowett—to interpret the biblical text *without* reference to creeds and controversies that were "of other times"—so stated, involved a fundamental historical error: for the faith of the creeds was not "of other times." The faith and the texts evolved together. There never were New Testament texts that did not witness to the faith that the creeds enshrine, and that faith never existed apart from the witness to it that the New Testament texts enshrine. Several theologians and biblical scholars over the last decade or so have emphasized the importance of perceiving the biblical story as the essential unifying theme of the Scriptures, and of the Rule of Faith as the key to understanding them.[4] This, as the writer to the Ephesians saw, is the true "mystery" of God's will: "to sum up all things in Christ" (Eph. 1:10)—and we recall that here "mystery (μυστήριον)" is virtually a technical term, meaning a divine secret that has been hidden but is now disclosed.[5]

This is not to say, however, that at this point our historical-critical disciplines become unimportant. Quite the reverse! Of course, there is always the temptation to say, "But is it not the story itself and the message that are important? If so, would it be a matter of concern if the story were a fiction? Does it matter if we see the resurrection of Christ as a work of the Holy Spirit in the human heart, rather than something that happened at a particular time and in a particular place?" But such questions are indeed a *temptation*—in the fullest and most dangerous sense of that word. The biblical story that we have been describing is a story about God's dealing with God's world and God's people *throughout history*, and therefore historical questions are not only appropriate but necessary. As Sir Edwyn Hoskyns and Noel Davey pointed out over three quarters of a century ago in a now classic study, whenever Christians confess the words of the Nicene faith, *and was incarnate*, they mark that "the Christian religion has its origin neither in general religious experience, nor in some peculiar esoteric mysticism, nor in a dogma."[6] Christian faith rests "upon a particular event in history…This is Christian orthodoxy, both Catholic and Protestant. In consequence, the Christian religion is not merely open to historical investigation, but demands it, and its piety depends on it."[7] Since Christianity is in this way an historical religion based upon the incarnation, so, as David Brown points out, "it matters hugely what sort of incarnation it was. How we consider the human Jesus to have lived will also fundamentally affect how in general we understand God's relation with the world and ourselves."[8] Orthodox Christianity cannot avoid having a concern for what really happened.

But then—what do we mean by "really"?

"The facts, ma'am, just the facts!" That, according to legend, is what Sergeant Joe Friday regularly said to emotional female witnesses in the course of the 1950s crime drama, *Dragnet.* In point of fact he never did say it, any more than Sherlock Holmes ever said, "elementary, my dear Watson," or Ilsa Lund said, "Play it again, Sam" in *Casablanca*—though they all said things like it, and the traditions, though inaccurate, do catch something of the characters and of the dramas with which they were involved. This may in itself suggest something to us about the meaning of the word "really." What, after all, do we learn from "just the facts"? What is a fact?

We might define "fact" as referring to documentary or other matter that can be verified, or has in the past been expertly tested, or is so reliably corroborated by other evidence as to render it persuasive.

> Fact is evidence, dated and proved and beyond all reasonable doubt genuine. I can walk into the Public Records Office in Kew and look at Shakespeare's Last Will and Testament of 1616. I may doubt that Shakespeare drew up the text himself; I may question the meaning of the various bequests in it; I may even believe that the man who signed the will was not the man who wrote the plays. But I cannot argue against the indisputable historical fact that this piece of parchment in front of me is the Last Will and Testament of William Shakespeare, Gent., of Stratford-upon-Avon in the county of Warwickshire, and that the shaky signature, the trembling autograph of a dying man, is his. This is a fact.[9]

So the Shakespearian scholar Graham Holderness: but of course his point is that the *unanswered* questions are about precisely the things he would *really* like to know—things that, if he did know them, would give him a much better sense than he can have now of what *really* happened.

But in the matter of biblical texts and the question of God we must go further. After all, Holderness's questions about Shakespeare are questions that we might in principle be able to answer, if we actually *knew* more facts—if we had the right evidence. We don't have such evidence, but we know what sort of evidence it would be, and we would probably recognize it if we came across it. Other kinds of questions, however, are open to no such possibility. If a young woman comes into my study and tells me that she has just met the most wonderful man in the world, and that he is called Charlie, she clearly presents me with a claim that would be hard for either of us to demonstrate or falsify—and for her, at least, it may be a very important claim, a claim that will give joy and significance to his life and hers, and lead to future generations who are to be lights of the world. All this is possible, but it cannot be demonstrated. On the other hand, if I discover on investigation that as a matter of ascertainable fact there *is* no man in her life called Charlie, then I may well question her sanity or her truthfulness. To that extent, her claim is open to critical investigation. Critical realism[10] demands that we confess the subjective element in all our observations. It also requires that we subject our observations to investigation where that is possible and appropriate.

As Christians we confess with the first disciples, "God raised Jesus from the dead." That is primarily a theological statement, and, as such, is neither verifiable nor falsifiable. God is not a proper subject for critical investigation: hence, as Diarmaid MacCulloch points out, "historians do not possess a prerogative to pronounce on the existence of God itself, any more than do (for example) biologists."[11] On the other hand, could critical investigation demonstrate that there never *was* such a person as Jesus of Nazareth, or that the first Christians had simply stolen the body and faked the resurrection (as some at least as early as the Gospel of Matthew were suggesting [Matt. 28:11-15]), then we should be obliged to question either their sanity or their honesty. I say this with confidence, since it appears to me that if one thing is historically certain, it is that the first Christians really had known a man called Jesus, really believed that his tomb was empty, and really believed that he had been raised from the dead. We may make of their conviction what we will, but the *fact* of it, in my view, can scarcely be denied by anyone with any historical sense. There is too much evidence for it.[12] To that extent, then, the origins of the Christian faith are indeed open to critical investigation...but *only* to that extent. Because of course in both cases—that of the young woman and that of the Christian confession—it is precisely what cannot be demonstrated, what cannot be shown to be either "fact" or "not fact," that is important and interesting.

There is a powerful moment in one of C. S. Lewis's children's books—*The Voyage of the Dawn Treader*. The children who are Lewis's main characters are in the magical world of Narnia, and there they meet an Old Man who turns out to be a star.

> "In our world," said Eustace, "a star is a huge ball of flaming gas."
> "Even in your world, my son, that is not what a star is, but only what it is made of."[13]

So with a human being: almost 99 percent of the mass of the human body is made up of six elements: oxygen, carbon, hydrogen, nitrogen, calcium, and phosphorus. About 0.85 percent is composed of five elements: potassium, sulfur, sodium, chlorine, and magnesium. The tiny remainder consists of trace elements, such as fluorine, which hardens dental enamel. Is *that*, then, what a human being *is*? Of course not! It is only what a human being is made of! Likewise, true history, real history, is so much more than we can touch, see, or verify experimentally, and a history that confines itself to those things is in Christian terms inevitably a false, distorted history. *True* history needs therefore not only to record facts, but also to go beyond facts, to transcend them, and this is what the biblical writers do. Prophetic and apostolic memory looks back into history and sees truths that it did not see at the time: so the Fourth Evangelist, meditating on and deepening his understanding of the life of Christ:

> What first were guessed as points, I now knew stars,
> And named them in the Gospel I have writ.[14]

Thus, for the implied audience of these texts, the truth that counts is never just a matter of the narrative's factual accuracy. As Catherine Playoust and Ellen Bradshaw Aitken remind us, speaking in particular of the canonical birth narratives and the *Protevangelium of James*, "Early Christians who were sympathetic to the content and purpose of these works would have considered them neither fictional stories about fictional people, nor nonfictional stories about people of no great note, but revelatory texts about the key figure of Jesus and certain people closely associated with him. The preservation and transmission of these texts as holy writings demonstrates that a sufficient number of followers of Jesus valued them in this way in the early centuries. (At least a few in the ancient audiences would have recognized that imaginative development of traditions had taken place, to a greater or lesser extent, but this need not have impeded for them the capacity of the texts to convey religious truth.)"[15]

Markus Bockmuehl makes the point in the opening pages of his interesting little book, *Seeing the Word*.[16] He considers a miniature of *St. Luke Painting the Virgin and Child*, painted at some time during the 1460s by Simon Marmion or members of his workshop. In the picture, the saint sits at his easel, and we can see both his "model" and the portrait he has painted. The "model" is a rather realistic seeming Northern European girl from the Low Countries. She looks a little tired, and the child is pulling cheerfully at her dress—all in all, a youthful mother somewhat exhausted by the taxing demands of a bouncing infant! On the head of each there is indeed a faint halo, but you have to look hard to see it. What, then, of Luke's "portrait"? It certainly resembles the originals in various ways—dress, the color of the Virgin's hair, and so—but it is also strikingly different. The scene is now one of restful contemplation, as would be appropriate in an icon of the Virgin Mother of God. In other words, what Marmion has given us is a portrait of the evangelist not merely as a conveyor of facts, but as a spiritual artist.

> Before Luke are a mother and child who, in the disarmingly unremarkable humanity of their demeanor, appear at one level like a thousand others, as if arbitrarily invited in from the street to sit for the artist on this particular fine spring morning. And yet Luke's piercing eye perceives the deeper reality of what is barely hinted at in the faint haloes of his models: his

gaze and brush reveal the truth that this is none other than the Mother of the Divine Word made flesh.[17]

Is such an approach simply unrealistic? Does it mean overlooking the way things actually are, the real Mary? Not in the least! John Gatta, in his beautiful and profound little book *The Transfiguration of Christ and Creation,* reflects on the synoptic narratives of the Transfiguration:

> To see the world transfigured need not, and indeed should not, mean that we look on it naively oblivious to its pain. Neither does attentiveness to the innate glory of things force us to pretend that we already inhabit an end time where sin, ugliness, and affliction have been erased. Transfiguration looks towards God's ultimate, all-encompassing redemption without overlooking life's sorrow. In mystical terms, it means seeing beneath apparently solid surfaces into the hidden life of things, or seeing with the eye of love.[18]

This is how the prophetic and apostolic perception works throughout Scripture. The eye of fleshly observation looks at the world and sees chaos, nature "red in tooth and claw." Paul looks on the same world with the eye of an apostle, and sees what that chaos means: "the whole creation waits with eager longing for the revealing of the children of God" (Rom. 8:19).

The point is, reality perceived by the eye of faith—by the prophetic eye, the apostolic eye—is *always* more than "the facts, just the facts" can convey. The fundamentalist reader of the Bible is scandalized by this, and insists that faith's reality *must* have been clear and identical with what could be seen and measured. The well-informed skeptic smiles in the superiority of a fuller knowledge (fortified, naturally, by the ever-blessed hermeneutic of suspicion) and since what could be seen and measured was evidently so much more *ordinary* than what is claimed by faith, dismisses faith's claims as fantasy. Fundamentalist and skeptic alike are making the same mistake. The creature is not merely what it is made of. The creature is indeed dust, but it is beloved dust. And history—what "really" happened—is always more than what scientific discipline would regard as "facts." Of course Jesus "suffered under Pontius Pilate." That is a fact. But the meaning of the fact, what was really happening in and through that no doubt bloody and disgusting scene on a hill outside Jerusalem—those things will only be apparent to prophetic and apostolic imagination, to the eye of faith. If we are to read the Bible and engage its matter at all, then we must try to make the prophetic and apostolic imagination our own.[19]

(2) THE DIFFERENT VOICES AND THEIR DIFFERENT ACCOUNTS OF THE HISTORY

As the biblical tradition grew and developed over the thousand or so years of its evolving, its memories interacted with each other, with new ideas building themselves into old stories so that the stories were understood in new ways and fresh contexts. "We have," as Walter Ong says, "no other book got together as a whole out of a communal memory the way the Bible has been."[20] One result of this is that the different texts of the Bible often represent different attitudes toward the overall story, different emphases, and sometimes-conflicting theologies. Our first task as biblical scholars was to listen to each of the many voices that the Bible contains: but as we consider them *in relation to each other*, we cannot avoid perceiving that, while they indeed witness to parts of a single story, they do not all say the same things about that story or take the same attitudes. Sometimes they appear explicitly to develop or amend or even contradict each other. In other words, and as David Brown puts it, "tradition does not develop in a single straight line but by exploring a range of possibilities, some of which are subsequently discarded."[21] So Walter Brueggemann in his *Theology of the Old Testament* has taught us to recognize a *plurality* of faith affirmations and interpretative communities, and hence to speak of Israel's "testimony" and "countertestimony."[22] No doubt some elements in this debate should be seen as a result of Israel's and the Church's coming to new understanding of God over time. There are elements in both Old and New Testaments that insist on being interpreted diachronically rather than synchronically. Cases in point would be the relationship between the Mosaic tradition as presented in Exodus, Leviticus, and Numbers, and then as later presented in Deuteronomy; and Davidic tradition as in the books of Samuel and Kings, and later in the books of Chronicles. In both cases, imagination has worked on the original traditions and in some respects transformed them. Our penchant for the historical-critical naturally leads us to prefer the older source—it is more "original." But theological reflection can hardly be satisfied with such a simple conclusion. Perhaps the version of the commandments in Exodus 20:17, which appears to rate a man's wife as less important to him than his house, is more primitive than that in Deuteronomy 5:21, which reverses the order. Perhaps it is not.[23] But in any case, what we have here, and in Deuteronomy as a whole,[24] is an example of what Brueggemann calls "the dynamic of the Torah," whereby "the

Torah insists on a regular, authoritative restatement in order to keep the command of Yahweh current to the time, place, and circumstance in which the people of the command live."

> Moses surely believes that there is no circumstance in which Yahweh does not will something concrete. But all of that is not known ahead of time. It is known only in the moment of new utterance "today" when given by the authorized interpreter.[25]

A particularly striking example of the Scripture's offering testimony and counter-testimony is its debate over the kind of relationship there should be between the people of God and those outside the people of God. Some voices in the Old Testament tell a story of Israel's relationship to the other nations, which is to be no relationship at all: the nations have nothing to do with Israel and Israel must have nothing to do with them, for the Lord will destroy them before her (e.g., Deut. 7:1-4, 12:29-30, Joshua 24). Other voices tell us that Israel's vocation is to be a blessing to the nations, that the nations may act graciously toward Israel, and God's ultimate purpose is to be gracious to all (Gen. 12:1-3, Isa. 49:5-6; cf. Ps. 67:1-7, 86:9-10, 117:1-2, Eccles. 44:19-21).

Mutatis mutandis, we find in the New Testament parallel tensions. The Seer of Revelation tells a story of God's apparent rejection and torment of vast numbers of people (including Jews) who have never, presumably, even heard of Jesus or Christianity, simply on the grounds that they are not Christians (Rev. 20:7-15). Other voices—notably the fourth evangelist at other points in his narrative and overwhelmingly the greater part of the Pauline tradition—tell us of a gracious promise that is to include *all* (John 12:32; Rom. 11:32, Eph. 1:10, Col 1:19). Indeed, in the end even the seer of Revelation seems finally to contradict himself on this question, for he concludes (according to the best text) with a universal promise: "may the grace of the Lord Jesus be with *all*" (Rev. 22:21). (The last verse of Revelation, which is also the last verse of the New Testament, is preserved in several textual variations, most of which would limit the seer's blessing to the church. Such variations were followed by the King James Version, Douay-Rheims, the Revised Version of 1884, and, surprisingly, the NRSV. But there can be little doubt that the shortest *and universal* version of the seer's blessing, witnessed by Alexandrinus and Jerome, is the earliest and correct reading: this is the version followed by the New American Bible, the French *Traduction Oecuménique de la Bible*, the Revised Version margin, the Spanish *Santa Biblia Reina-Walera 1995* margin, and the New English Bible margin[26]).

Another Old Testament example of testimony and counter-testimony would be the question as to whether or not Israel should have a king like other nations. There is a tension between the tradition of Moses and Sinai, and that of David and Jerusalem. Some voices tell us a story in which God's will for Israel is that her only king should be God (Judg. 8:22-23 cf. Hosea 13:9-11). Other voices tell us that God, even if reluctantly, does permit Israel to have a king like the nations around her, and will bless him (1 Sam. 8:11-18, 9:15-16, Ps. 89:3-4).[27]

In such matters as these it is the biblical scholar's task to discern the different voices and listen to them, relating them to the Scriptural narrative, the Rule of Faith, as a whole. Such a process of Scriptural study will in practice be a dialectic in which we work both ways, sometimes considering the parts in relation to the whole, sometimes the whole in relation to the parts.[28] What we must not do, however, is *ignore* or try to *disguise* the multiplicity of voices. Naturally we are tempted to follow such a course, since naturally we like easy and clear answers. Nevertheless, we must resist it. We must acknowledge all the voices, both in their own context and in their relationship to the overall "text" of the Scriptures, to the Rule of Faith. Will the attempt to discern this relationship involve problems?—"a problematic," as contemporary jargon likes to have it? Certainly it will! It will mean sometimes showing how these voices are reconciled, and sometimes how one voice is preferred to another.

In some cases this preference is already indicated within the canons of Scripture, Scripture itself making clear which tradition is to be discarded. Thus, although the story of God's "no" to the nations continues to be told, it is clear, I think, that in the Scriptures taken as a whole, the story of God's *grace* to the nations and therefore of Israel's positive relationship to them is privileged over the more violent narrative. It runs deeper and longer. It is presented as God's first word over not only the nations but the entire creation (Gen. 1:31), and it is God's last word, as at 2 Chronicles 36:23—the closing word of the Jewish canon—and, as we have seen, Revelation 22:21, the closing word of the Christian. There are, moreover, moments in this particular debate where a voice on one side seems to be aware of voices on the other and deliberately to correct them. One such instance is in the tale of Jonah's prophecy that Nineveh will "be overthrown" (נֶהְפָּכֶת: we might render it, "will be turned upside down") (3:4). The prophecy is indeed fulfilled, but, to the prophet's irritation, not by Nineveh's destruction but by Nineveh's repentance, which God accepts (Jonah 3 3:4-4:11).[29] Another such challenge involves Ezra and Nehemiah's exclusivism in their expulsion of the foreign women (Ezra 10:17-44, Neh.

23-31). This narrative is confronted by the story of Ruth the Moabite; and the challenge is made especially blatant at the end of that story, where we learn that the foreign wife whom Ezra and Nehemiah would have expelled is not only a proselyte who has freely chosen to take refuge under the wings of the Lord God of Israel (Ruth 2:12) but who will also, as it turns out, be King David's great-grandmother! (Ruth 4:13-22)[30]

Another issue that I have mentioned, the issue as to whether Israel should only have the Lord God as her king or whether there should be a human king, the tension between the Mosaic Sinai and Davidic Zion, is not, I would argue, finally worked out in the Old Testament at all, but finds reconciliation in the New, where Jesus is seen both as the prophet like Moses, the fulfillment of the Law, and as the son of David, the fulfiller of the Messianic hope.[31]

In other cases, preference of one voice over another is *not* entirely clear from the texts of either Old or New Testaments, but has come to be indicated over time by what Walter Brueggemann calls "the reading community"—although I would prefer to call it "the listening community"—that is, the church. An example of that would be an issue that I have not so far mentioned: the issue of slavery. There are passages in both Old and New Testaments that imply tolerance of that institution, and there are others that undermine it. It took a long time—so long as to be almost within living memory— for the church to decide on this question: but the church *did* finally decide, and now I imagine that no Christian of any stripe would regard slavery as acceptable. It may be argued— and I would say argued correctly—that the seeds of the current view of things are clearly present in the Scriptures. Paul's assertion that Philemon shall receive back his slave "no longer as a slave, but as a brother," and the baptismal assertion that in Christ "there is neither bond nor free" surely point in that direction. Yet it took many centuries for the church to see that, and the fact that there is a plurality of voices in Scripture was one reason why it took so long.

A particular and very important instance of slowness in coming to decision is the issue of the church's attitude toward the Jews. As we have already pointed out in discussing the hermeneutic of suspicion, there are certainly parts of the New Testament that suggest a negative attitude toward the Jews, and no doubt this negativity springs from the break between church and synagogue that occurred in the first century, and is properly understood as a family quarrel. The New Testament writers also represent, of course, a situation in which the synagogue would generally have had the upper hand, and so they doubtless speak out of some sense of apprehension and oppression. All this must be continually spelled out and brought home to the church of the twenty-first century by the biblical scholar, if the church is not, as has alas often happened in the past, to make the mistake of transmuting this first-century family quarrel into a contemporary anti-Semitism.

In still other cases, Christians continue to debate and disagree about which voice is to be preferred—or even whether there is actually a difference of voices. In this situation, biblical scholars *as biblical scholars* must point out the issues, and possibly suggest why Christians of intelligence and goodwill are at odds over their proper resolution: which does not mean, of course, that biblical scholars may not also have their own views as to the rights and wrongs of the matter, and where the church should go. In the last thirty or so years of the twentieth century, and the first decade of the twenty-first, issues surrounding patriarchy and homosexuality have been obvious examples of this.

All that granted, we must in the end again stress that *the fact that there is a plurality of voices telling the story does not mean that there is a plurality of stories.* Yes, says Brueggemann of the Old Testament, there are different witnesses. "Yet taken together," he adds, "these witnesses, different as they are, advocate a Yahweh-version of reality that is strongly in conflict with other versions of reality and other renderings of truth that have been shaped without reference to Yahweh and that determinedly propose a reality and truth that is Yahweh-free."[32] Exactly. And in somewhat the same way, we have also in the New Testament a plurality of voices offering different emphases, at certain points in conflict with one another. And here, too, different though they may be, the voices are united in witnessing to a version of reality that is centered upon God our Father and the Lord Jesus Christ: a version of reality that is therefore sharply in conflict with any version developed without reference to God our Father and the Lord Jesus Christ.

It will be clear that for all their sprawling diversity, I do believe the Scriptures as a whole have coherence: a theme and a direction. I am taken with James Sanders's comparison with the Cathedral of Our Lady of Chartres: the product of a long process, in design and even in some of its contents, it is hard to categorize, save as does one of its most ardent admirers: "a mess."[33] Yet with the Bible as with Chartres Cathedral, the whole is infinitely greater than the parts, and its glory is the One who has chosen to be witnessed through it. As for inspiration in Scripture, as for the work of the Holy Spirit in the process of its creation and in the results of that process, it must be looked for, as I have said elsewhere, in every part of that process and its results,[34] from the first telling of a tale or grasping at a piece of (quite possibly pagan) wisdom, to the latest believer who hears or reads and is thereby moved to attempt faith and obedience to the God of Israel. Northrop Frye said, "if the Bible is to be regarded as 'inspired' in any sense, sacred or secular, the editing and conflating and redacting and splicing and glossing and expurgating processes all have to be inspired too. There is no way of distinguishing the voice of God from the voice of the Deuteronomic redactor."[35] Exactly.

All of which brings us to our third task.

Notes

1. Northrop Frye, *The Great Code* xiii.
2. I have of course borrowed the phrase from my friend Robert D. Hughes III: and for it see his remarkable book, *Beloved Dust: Tides of the Spirit in the Christian Life* (New York: Continuum, 2008).
3. See my *Resurrection of the Messiah* (Oxford: Oxford University Press, 2011), especially 69–70.
4. See e.g., Bernard Sesboüé, *L'évangile et la Tradition* (Paris: Bayard, 2008), ET *Gospel and Tradition*, Patricia Kelly, transl. (Miami: Convivium, 2012); Robert W. Jenson, *Canon and Creed* (Louisville, Ky.: Westminster John Knox, 2010); cf. Paul Ricoeur, "Toward a Hermeneutic of the Idea of Revelation" in Ricoeur, *Essays on Biblical Interpretation*, Lewis S. Mudge, ed. (Philadelphia: Fortress, 1990), 77–81; Ricouer, "Interpretative Narrative," David Pellauer, trans., in *The Book and the Text: The Bible and Literary Theory*, Regina Schwartz, ed. (Oxford: Basil Blackwell, 1990), 236–57; see also Christopher Bryan, *And God Spoke: The Authority of the Bible for the Church Today* (Lanham, Maryland: Cowley, 2002) 10–13, 25–26.
5. See BDAG, μυστήριον, 1 and 2; also *TDNT* 4.817–822.

6. Sir Edwyn Hoskyns and Noel Davey, *The Riddle of the New Testament* (London: Faber and Faber, 1931; rev. 1936), 12.
7. Ibid. See also the carefully nuanced observations of Hans W. Frei, "Theological Reflections on the Accounts of Jesus' Death and Resurrection" in Frei, *Theology and Narrative: Selected Essays*, George Hunsinger and William C. Placher, eds. (New York and Oxford: Oxford University Press, 1991), 45–94 esp. 86–87 (originally published in *The Christian Scholar* **49**: 4 [1966] 263–306).
8. David Brown, *Tradition and Imagination: Revelation and Change* (Oxford: Oxford University Press, 1999), 275.
9. Holderness, *Nine Lives of William Shakespeare* 6.
10. On critical realism, see N. T. Wright, *Christian Origins and the Question of God, 1. The New Testament and the People of God* (London: SPCK, 1992), 32–46 and passim.
11. Diarmaid MacCulloch, *A History of Christianity: The First Three Thousand Years* (London: Allen Lane, 2010) / *Christianity: The First Three Thousand Years* (New York: Viking, 2010), 11.
12. See Christopher Bryan, *The Resurrection of the Messiah* (Oxford: Oxford University Press, 2012) 163 and passim.
13. C. S. Lewis, *The Voyage of the Dawn Treader* (London: Geoffrey Bles, 1952), 189.
14. Robert Browning, "A Death in the Desert," 155–57.
15. Catherine Playoust and Ellen Bradshaw Aitken, "The Leaping Child: Imagining the Unborn in Early Christian Literature," in Vanessa R. Sasson and Jane Marie Law, eds. *Imagining the Fetus: The Unborn in Myth, Religion, and Culture.* AAR Cultural Criticism Series (Oxford; Oxford University Press, 2009), 160.
16. Marcus Brockmuehl, *Seeing the Word: Refocusing New Testament Study* (Grand Rapids, Mich.: Baker Academic, 2006).
17. Bockmuehl, *Seeing the Word*, 18.
18. John Gatta, *The Transfiguration of Christ and Creation* (Eugene, Oregon: Wipf and Stock, 2011), 41.
19. See Adrian Walker, "Fundamentalism and the Catholicity of Truth," in *Communio* **29** (2002), 22–25.
20. Ong, *Interfaces*, 232.

21. David Brown, *Discipleship and Imagination: Christian Tradition and Truth* (Oxford: Oxford University Press, 2000), 31.

22. Walter Brueggemann, *Theology of the Old Testament: Testimony, Dispute, Advocacy* (Minneapolis: Fortress, 1997), vii, xv–xvi, and passim.

23. See Brevard S. Childs, *The Book of Exodus* (Louisville, Ky.: Westminster John Knox, 1974), 427.

24. δευτερονόμιον: that is, δεύτερος, "second," which may imply mere repetition, but may also, as plainly here, imply a fresh version.

25. Brueggemann, *Theology of the Old Testament*, 183.

26. See Bruce M. Metzger, *A Textual Commentary on the Greek New Testament: A Companion Volume to the United Bible Societies Greek New Testament,* 3rd edition (London and New York: United Bible Societies, 1975) 766–67.

27. See Paul D. Hanson, *The Diversity of Scripture* (Philadelphia: Fortress, 1982) 24–26; Christopher Bryan, *Render to Caesar: Jesus, the Early Church, and the Roman Superpower* (Oxford: Oxford University Press, 2005), 17–21, 135–36.

28. See B. David Napier, *From Faith to Faith: Essays on Old Testament Literature* (New York: Harper, 1955), xix.

29. See Jack M. Sasson, *Jonah*, AB 24B (New York: Doubleday, 1990), 234–35, 236–37, 345 n.34.

30. On the closing genealogy (Ruth 4:18–22), which forms an *inclusio* with 1:1–5 and is (whatever its origin) part of the Masoretic text, against many commentators I find most persuasive André LaCocque, *Ruth*, K. C. Hanson, transl. (Minneapolis: Fortress, 2004 [2004]), 147–54.

31. See Jon D. Levenson's splendid *Sinai and Zion: An Entry to the Jewish Bible* (New York: Winston Press, 1985)—although, as is evident, I do not entirely agree with his understanding of the New Testament's attitude to the tension.

32. Brueggemann, *Theology of the Old Testament*, xvii.

33. John James, *Chartres: The Masons who Built a Legend* (London: Routledge and Kegan Paul, 1982), 9; cited Sanders, *Sacred Story to Sacred Text*, 4.

34. Christopher Bryan, *And God Spoke* (Cambridge, Mass.: Cowley, 1989) 60–61; cf. Robert W. Jenson, *Systematic Theology* (Oxford and New York: Oxford University Press, 1997-99), 2. 276.

35. Frye, *Great Code*, 203.

IX

THE THIRD TASK: SO WHAT NOW?

(1) WHY WE MUST ASK THE QUESTION

Our earlier question, "how do the individual voices of Scripture relate to scripture as a whole?" inevitably brought us, contrary to what Benjamin Jowett expected, into considering the Bible in relation to the Rule of Faith, and so to the creeds. But the creeds are not statements merely about the past. They do not say, "the early church believed" or "the apostles believed," but "I believe" and "we believe." In other words, consideration of the Bible in relation to the creeds leads inexorably to our third question: how does the Bible relate to the life of the church up to and including today?[1]

Looking back with the benefit of a century and a half of hindsight, we may well think that (as are so many of us) Jowett was right in what he affirmed and wrong in what he denied. He was, as I have suggested, at least to some extent right about the need to approach the Bible as we would any other book. He was also right about the perils involved in looking for answers to our own questions from texts that were written without any conception of such questions. One has only to turn to the various ways in which the Bible was appealed to in order to defend slavery in the eighteenth and nineteenth centuries, or to the utter nonsense that is still put forward about "the Bible and the ordination of women to the priesthood" or "the Bible and homosexuality" to see that there are such perils: the continuing need for Jowett's cautions is obvious, as is the quicksand into which we stray when we ignore them.

But Jowett was surely wrong in imagining that as a result, the task may not or should not be undertaken—or even that it can be avoided. The meanings a text has for us are *always* affected by what we bring to it, by our own particular understandings and experiences, that is, by our personal, inner "texts," conscious or unconscious. How very differently Isaiah 53 or the first verse of Psalm 22—"My God, my God, why hast thou forsaken me?"—must resonate with a Jew who reads in the light of the Holocaust and a gentile Christian who reads in the light of Jesus' passion! And since every person who comes to these texts is unique and has a particular history, there is always the possibility for new meaning. This is true of all great texts, and is therefore true of biblical texts.[2]

Some Christians seem to find this threatening, but it seems to me entirely appropriate that God's revelation must always be capable of unfolding for us new meaning.[3] For the fact that our knowledge of God is as yet incomplete does not mean that we have no knowledge, or that there is no God to be known, or that the effort to know more is not proper, or that it will not be rewarded. I have long delighted in a rabbinic tradition that those who study Scripture faithfully in this life get to study it in the Age to Come, in the Light of the Shekinah. A Jewish friend tells me that this is to say the Scriptures are inexhaustible, and always capable of giving us new meaning. To which I happily reply, Amen!

So—how, then, shall we tackle this third task: the perilous activity of relating the biblical texts to the ongoing life of the church? There is a sense in which we begin that task every time we listen to the gospel read in church and ask what it means. For as a Christian of the twenty-first century, I am already woven into *that* "text"—the twenty-first century church "text"—and inevitably I bring it with me to my consideration. So there is a sense in which I am already beginning to perform our third task—relating the Bible to the church of today—just by listening to the reading.[4] Again, the texts themselves from time to time thrust us in this direction: as does the "this day" of Luke and Hebrews (Luke 2:11, Heb. 4:7). In one sense this speaks of a day in the past; yet the form in which it is presented, especially in Hebrews—"saying in David after so long a time, 'This day'"—indicates that if the words of Luke and the writer to the Hebrews were ever true, then they must *still* be true. Salvation history is history, a story of the past: but it is a past that is not over, and it is about things that continue to be true *now*—and even to the end of the world (cf. Rom. 4:23-25).

It is sometimes suggested that the very fact of our historical study of the Bible, the very kind of study that we have advocated as our first task, makes it impossible for us to perform our third, and relate it to the twenty-first century church.[5] Richard Hays in *The Moral Vision of the New Testament*[6] gives a poignant example of this view. He was leading a seminar on the Bible in Kansas, in the course of which he had persuaded a pastor (correctly, in my opinion) that a major concern for Paul in Romans was to explain the relationship of Jew and gentile in God's Providence, and to show that God's grace in the gospel does not abrogate God's promises to Israel. The pastor replied, "Professor Hays, you've convinced me that you're right about Romans, but now I don't see how I can preach from it any more. Where I serve out in Western Kansas, Israel's fate isn't a burning issue for my people, and there's not a Jew within a hundred miles of my church." By the same token, Mark Nanos, in his generous and thoughtful critique of my own book, *Preface to Romans*, put a number of salient questions to me, one of which was this: granted I see

Romans as relevant to contemporary preachers, does not my approach risk "confining the results of [my] analysis to the interpretative concerns of another time, place, and person than the mid-first century, Cenchreae and Rome, or Paul?"[7] In other words, if we succeed in locating Paul properly in the first century, have we lost him for twenty-first-century Kansas? Alternatively, if we see in him elements that are relevant to the situation in twenty-first-century Kansas, have we lost him for first-century Rome?

I concede that both questions do point to a real problem. The issue was powerfully described in 1936 by the great Homer scholar Milman Parry in a paper on "The Historical Method in Literary Criticism."[8]

> When one trained in this method, while still staying in the past, turns his eyes back to his own time, he cannot prevent a certain feeling of fear—not for the fact that he has become a ghost in the past, but because of what he sees in the person of his living self. For in the past, where his ghostly self is, he finds that men do the opposite of what he has been doing: they by their literature turn the past into the present, making it the mirror for themselves, and as a result the past as it is expressed in their literature has a hold upon them which shows up the flimsiness of the hold which our past literature has upon ourselves.

Parry goes on to illustrate this by referring to a passage from Robert Wood's *Essay on the Genius of Homer*, published in 1767.

> There is a famous passage in the twelfth book of the *Iliad* in which Sarpedon, the ally of the Trojans, calls upon his friend Glaucus to follow him to the assault on the Greek Wall: "If after

escaping this war we were to become ageless and deathless, then would I not fight myself in the front ranks, nor urge you into the battle which gives men glory. But there are hazards of death beyond counting which stand above us, and which no man can escape or dodge. So let us go forward: which shall give glory to some man, or some man will give glory to us.". . . .

Robert Wood says that in 1762, at the end of the Seven Years' War, being then Under-Secretary of State, he was directed to wait upon the President of the Council, Lord Granville, a few days before he died, with the preliminary articles of the Treaty of Paris. "I found him so languid that I proposed postponing my business for another time; but he insisted that I should stay, saying it could not prolong his life to neglect his duty, and repeating the following passage out of Sarpedon's speech, he dwelled with particular emphasis on the third line, 'Then would I not fight myself in the front ranks,' which called to his mind the distinguished part he had taken in public affairs." And then Lord Granville recited to himself in Greek the lines which I just gave you in translation.[9]

Parry's point was this: because of his training in historical method, he could read those verses with an understanding that Lord Granville could never have had. Parry knew, for example, that for those who first sang and heard Sarpedon's words, they were an assertion in heroic terms of their own way of life. They offered a sanction and an ideal for it. They saw no great difference between what Sarpedon said and did, and the things they themselves aspired to say and do. They had no desire to learn "how things really were" in the past: they treated the past as a mirror for themselves. Hence, its hold on them was very powerful. That is how Homer was heard for centuries and that, mutatis mutandis, was how Lord Granville was still hearing him two-and-a-half thousand years later. Therefore, Parry pointed out, Granville was in a sense closer to the text as the ancients would have received it than was Parry himself, for all Parry's scholarship—*and partly because of it.*

What shall we say to this? I concede that Parry does point to a real change in our understanding and so to a real problem: the problem raised by Nanos and the pastor from Kansas whom I cited earlier. Yet all three, in my view, so state the problem as to overstate it. Yes, it is true that we no longer assume that what we find in ancient authors writing about their particular situations may be applied without remainder to our own situations just because they seem to suit. Yes, it is true that an imaginative leap is required to go between Homer's situation or Paul's situation and ours.

Nevertheless, the leap is not impossible. It may be rather hard for academics like myself, who generally lead rather sheltered lives, to realize it, but the fact is, there are still many people—soldiers and firefighters and police, for example—who frequently choose "to fight in the front ranks" because they would rather do their duty than be safe, and despite all that separates them from Homer, they could still make those words of Sarpedon's their own, just as Lord Granville did. As for Saint Paul's situation and ours, the human heart is as prone in twenty-first-century Europe and North America as it was in Paul's first-century Rome to the arrogance and self-righteousness that made it difficult for Roman Jews and gentiles to "welcome one another, therefore, just as Christ welcomed [them], for the glory of God." (Rom. 15.7) That alone makes Paul's concerns in the Letter to the Romans relevant to the twenty-first century, for it is a point where the "text"—the texture—in which he found himself and the "text" in which we find ourselves *do* interweave.

We can, if we choose, claim that the pastness of the past shields us from its challenges: and so we may, like Charles Williams's Damaris Tighe in *The Place of the Lion*, excuse ourselves from taking seriously anything that ancient writers say to us.[10] But if we do, we indulge in an illusion that is at least as dangerous and ridiculous as the assumption that writers in the past simply wrote to people and situations that were the same as ours. The fact is, millions of people in virtually every culture all over the world continue to perform, watch, and be enthralled by writers from other ages and other cultures. They do not do this simply because they find in the works of these authors interesting historical exercises that are nonetheless finally irrelevant to their own lives or else finally incomprehensible. Quite the contrary! Faced by Euripides's *Hecuba*, why is it that I am at once captivated and appalled? It is because, even though the world in which I live is very different from Euripides's world, it is still a world in which nations are conquered and enslaved, where crooks like Euripides's Polymestor betray and murder for money, where fine-talking politicians like his Odysseus are hypocrites and fakes and get away with it, where honest men like his Talthybius can see what is wrong but don't know how to change it, and where men like his Agamemnon occasionally manage to do the right thing almost in spite of themselves. And although my social location is different from theirs, might I not, with a little effort of imagination, still perceive how the present experience of Palestinians, oppressed in their own land, or the experience of enslaved African Americans in the United States, might resonate with the story of Hecuba and the other enslaved Trojan women?[11] And indeed these connections were brought home to me quite recently, by a production of Marilyn Nelson's translation, in which the part of Hecuba was stunningly played by the African American actress Tarashai Lee.[12]

To sum up: we resonate with great writers of the past because they portray the human lot. However different from theirs our experience of that lot may be, we all still share it. We are all still subject to things we cannot control, and we all still die. To that extent at least—and it is hardly a trivial extent—our "texts" interweave.

So much may be said in general terms. When it comes to the matter of a Christian scholar studying the Scriptures, however, the matter must be stated more sharply, for such a person is not simply in the position of, say, the secular academic studying Euripides. Why? Because Christian scholars studying the Bible are *not*, essentially, in a different community of interpretation from those whom they study. They are still members of the same family. The past history of the people of God is *our* past—even, I may claim, *my* past. The biblical writers' worlds were different from mine and I had better not forget it. Nevertheless, a sound theology should remind me that what I have in common with those writers is far more important than anything that divides me from them, for what I have in common with them is not only, as with Euripides, our common humanity, but also our common fellowship in the people of God. In other words, my "text" as an individual and our "texts" as a community do engage with the biblical writers' "texts" at numerous points, both personally and theologically. As I have said, their "today" is by its very nature also bound up with my "today."

2. THE SCRIPTURES AS INTERPRETATIVE NARRATIVE

Paul Ricoeur claimed, I believe correctly, that some narratives are by their nature "interpretative," by which he meant "the ideological interpretation these narratives wish to convey is not superimposed on the narrative by the narrator but is, instead, incorporated into the very strategy of the narrative."[13] So "the juncture between exegesis and theology, before being a work of interpretation applied *to* the text, already functions *in* the text if this text is a narrative with an interpretive function."[14] In other words, one might say that our experience with these stories is not so much that we succeed in relating them to our lives as that they insist on relating themselves to us. The stories of Alcestis, Psyche, Hecuba, and Oedipus are all, in their different ways, examples of such narrative. I do not follow what seems to be Ricouer's further claim, which is (if I understand him correctly) that *only* such poetic discourse can reveal God to us.[15] I would insist, on the contrary, that Christianity avoids being a merely gnostic religion precisely because it insists that the story it tells is also rooted in history. Nonetheless, Ricouer's insight about the interpretative function of some narratives resonates with the way in which certain narratives affect me, and especially do I find that to be true of the biblical narratives. Nor, evidently, am I alone in this: "when a story is great enough," the playwriter and novelist Dorothy Sayers wrote, "any honest craftsman may succeed in producing something not altogether unworthy, because the greatness is in the story, and does not need to borrow anything from the craftsman...I am a writer and I know my trade; and I say that this"—Sayers was writing of the story of the life of Christ as presented in the gospels—"is a very great story indeed, and deserves to be taken seriously."[16]

Thus, Erich Auerbach in *Mimesis*, and then more fully Robert Alter in *The Art of Biblical Narrative*,[17] show how the narrative structure of the Old Testament as it stands (irrespective of the history of those structures and texts as historical and textual criticism may imagine them to have been) stimulates theological reflection. It points to "the enactment of God's purposes in historical events." This enactment is complicated, however, by narrators' constant awareness of two tensions. One is a tension between God's plan and history—that is to say, between God's promise and its apparent non-fulfillment in what actually happens. The other is the tension between what God wills, God's gracious providence for humanity, and human disobedience, "the refractory nature of man."

> If one may presume at all to reduce great achievements to a common denominator, it might be possible to say that the depth with which human nature is imagined in the Bible is a function of its being conceived as caught in the powerful interplay of this double dialectic between design and disorder, providence and freedom.[18]

I would remark that such characteristics mark also the gospel narratives, and in particular the narratives of Jesus' passion and resurrection—that is, the foundational narratives of the New Testament and the heart of the Christian kerygma. So they work on us in the same way. And these two narratives taken together, Old and New Testaments, constitute, as we have noted, the basis of the Rule of Faith and the creeds of the universal church.

Narrative, by its very nature, is about what happened. It is about the past, and therefore about what is gone. Even the fairy tales' "and they all lived happily ever after" does not avoid this, for the past—"they *lived*"—still burdens us with the knowledge that this is not now. It is no more. It is dead, and what we have in the story is its monument. Many poets and writers have, of course, been aware of this, as Shakespeare, celebrating a beauty that can have no plea "against the wreckful siege of battering days" sees nonetheless that his own poem can be a memorial, "that in black ink my love may still shine bright" (*Sonnets* 65).

There is, however, a device—and perhaps we should think of it as more than a device, perhaps even as an insight—by which some narratives go some way to escape this pastness: it is by an ending that refuses to be an ending, but thrusts forward into the hearers' present, even into their future. Sometimes this is only hinted at, as by narratives that end in marriage and with a dance: for by its very nature marriage must remind us of God's eternal covenant and a dance must remind us, even if we hardly know it, of the everlasting dance. I think of staged performances that end in this way—of Shakespeare's *As You Like It* and *Much Ado About Nothing*, or Handel's *Giulio Cesare*. This last is particularly striking, since with the historical-critical part of our minds we know perfectly well, as Handel and his librettist certainly knew, that historically the marriage of Cleopatra and Caesar was by no means the beginning of an era of peace and joy. Yet in the staged opera it has clearly become that, and we leave the theater or switch off the Blu-ray player with our hearts open to a future in which there is peace and reconciliation.

Sometimes this thrust from the pastness of the narrative past becomes explicit. Shakespeare's Prospero comes forward at the end of *The Tempest* and states that he *has* no good future—or at least, he has none unless a condition be fulfilled, *which the audience might fulfill*:

> *Unless I be relieved by prayer,*
> *Which pierces so that it assaults*
> *Mercy itself and frees all faults.*
> *As you from crimes would pardoned be,*
> *Let your indulgence set me free.*

In other words, the story of Prospero is not over, and the play is clearly asking us to understand that. In this closing moment Prospero steps out of the imagined past into a present and future hope that are also our present and future hope: we leave the theater imaginatively aware that we are linked with him in a common destiny that points to all our futures.

The final of C. S. Lewis's seven Narnia books, *The Last Battle*, ends by pointing forward even as it speaks in the past tense:

> And for us this is the end of all the stories, and we can most truly say that they all lived happily ever after.

—so Lewis plays with the conventional ending of a fairy narrative, even as he transmutes it into something different—

> But for them it was only the beginning of the real story. All their life in this world and all their adventures in Narnia had only been the cover and the title page: now at last they were beginning Chapter One of the Great Story which no one on earth has read: which goes on for ever: in which every chapter is better than the one before.

Again, the story is not over and the text clearly requires us to understand that.

Obviously, there are many examples of such narratives claiming that their end is their true beginning, so I content myself, and conclude this section of my thoughts, by pointing to one of the greatest—the conclusion to Dante's *Paradiso*, where the poet's final question is taken up into a response that involves all time and eternity:

> *As the geometer intently seeks*
> *to square the circle, but he cannot reach,*
> *through thought on thought, the principle he needs,*
> *   so I searched that strange sight: I wished to see*
> *the way in which our human effigy*
> *suited the circle and found place in it—*
> *   and my own wings were far too weak for that.*
> *But then my mind was struck by a light that flashed*
> *and, with this light, received what it had asked.*
> *   Here force failed my high fantasy: but my*
> *desire and will were moved already—like*
> *a wheel revolving uniformly—by*
> *   the Love that moves the sun and the other stars.*
> *(Paradiso 33.133-45, Allen Mandelbaum, trans.)*[19]

Now this quality of ending with the beginning, of ending in a way that points us to our own futures, which are shared with the futures of the characters in the story, is supremely true of the Scriptural narrative, which always points forward. *Maranatha*! "Our Lord, come!" writes Saint Paul; and the New Testament as a whole closes with the same cry: "Come, Lord Jesus! The grace of our Lord Jesus Christ be with all. Amen." As Walter Ong said,

It is true that Jesus the Word has already come. But what the New Testament kerygma announces is not simply a repetition of the first coming. The text does not read, "Come back," but simply "Come." The new coming is not by any means a mere repetition of the first. It will not be like the first. No uroboros here. This the Bible itself makes clear. The second coming will be, "on the clouds of heaven," in judgment. And there are only two comings: the first, which prepares for the last, and the last, which is neither to repeat the first nor to finish off the first but rather to confirm and transmute the first and with it, everything, into the fullness of life.. .

The story of the Bible is not finished, nor is it meant to be.[20]

So the Gospel according to Saint Mark, replete with narrative brilliance, is never more so marked than in its conclusion: Jesus of Nazareth "is risen," which means therefore that he is "not here"—not, that is, confined by the tomb, the place of death. Rather, "he goes ahead," and "you will see him." What possibly shall be said to this, for it breaks open every kind of pastness that we have thought of, every kind of ending we have known, including death, which has always been an ending, by opening us to a totally new future? The only response that is appropriate is that which the women give: to flee the now irrelevant and outmoded place of death, to say nothing, and to be filled with awe: but a joyful awe since this is, against all present experience, "a happy ending" that is also a beginning.[21] And so it is, we must add, of the Bible's inseparable companion, the Rule of Faith, which is not in itself a story but implies a story, and is indeed meaningless without one: a story that begins at the commencement of time with God's creation of "heaven and earth," and finishes at the end of time with Christ's coming "in glory to judge the living and the dead," with his kingdom that "will have no end," and likewise with "the resurrection of the dead," and "the life of the world to come."

It is perhaps not irrelevant to this entire discussion that Dante called his work *Commèdia*— "comedy"—for in the last analysis only *commèdia* with its *svolgimento e finale solitamente lieti*—"customarily happy development and ending"—can express the Christian view of the universe.[22] Tragedy is, of course, understandable as an expression of human experience apart from God (or *apparently* apart from God). And indeed, as a European by culture, I find myself generally inclined to take a more tragic view of history than do my American friends—but I am, of course, talking of that history perceived as apart from God. In other words, I am talking of what Paul meant by σάρξ. And there is always a temptation to perceive history in this way so long as we regard it as only a linear unfolding of moments, rather than (as did an older Christianity) a continual participation in God's redeeming providence.[23] A narrative of events perceived as *within* the sphere of God's grace, judgment, and sovereignty remains essentially what Dante saw that it must be: *commèdia*. It perceives, as Carlo Maria Martini puts it in conversation with Umberto Eco, "that history has meaning and (to cite your own words) that one can 'love earthly reality and believe—with Charity—that there is still room for Hope.'"[24]

C.S. Lewis spoke of the biblical narrative, including the life of Jesus, as "myth made fact," meaning by myth, "not merely misunderstood history (as Euhemus thought) nor diabolical illusion (as some of the Fathers thought) nor priestly lying (as the philosophers of the Enlightenment thought) but, at its best, a real though unfocused gleam of divine truth falling on human imagination."[25] This being so, he noted of the life of Jesus that, "Just as God is none the less God by being Man, so the Myth remains Myth even when it becomes Fact. The story of Christ demands from us, and repays, not only a religious and historical but also an imaginative response. It is directed to the child, the poet, and the savage in us as well as to the conscience and the intellect."[26] As Ricoeur noted: for the interpretation is built into the very structure of the narrative. If we surrender ourselves to it, it will work on us.

But it does require surrender. This is a point made powerfully by Auerbach, initially speaking of the Old Testament, but evidently aware that what he says is equally true of the New:[27]

> The world of the Scriptures is not satisfied with claiming to be a historically true reality—it insists that it is the only real world, is destined for autocracy. All other scenes, issues, and ordinances have no right to appear independently of it, and it is promised that all of them, the history of all mankind, will be given their due place within its frame, will be subordinated to it. The Scripture stories do not, like Homer's, court our favor, they do not flatter us that they may please us and enchant us— they seek to subject us, and if we refuse to be subjected we are rebels.[28]

So we come full circle, and we find that, far from departing from the spirit of the texts, if we ask how they address our own lives and situations, we are actually in accord with that spirit, for the texts demand that response from us, and a soundly based and sensitive historical criticism—indeed, a truly "scientific" criticism—shows that to be so.

The Scriptures' "today" requires our "today."

3 THE EXERCISE OF CHRISTIAN IMAGINATION

The title that I originally gave to this book was *The Art of Interpreting Scripture in the Service of the Church.* I decided to change it because Cynthia Read of Oxford University Press (with whom I never argue) thought we needed something "zippier," and because even I had to admit it was a rather large title for a rather small book. Still, I was not wrong to speak of Scriptural interpretation as an art, involving exercise of the imagination, for such indeed it is: and that is why the word "art" still occurs in the subtitle. Even the most detached and careful historical critical study requires of us as much imagination, as well as much precision and care, as we can muster. Other areas and modes of interpreting and expounding give rein to other kinds of imagination, and a process of imagination has always been at work in the most important developments of Christian doctrine and ethics.

As regards doctrine, the two natures of Christ and the Trinitarian Godhead are, as the Fathers of the Church said they were, implicit in Scripture, and in that sense they are Scriptural doctrines. But what is *implicit* is by definition not *explicit.* It needed the impact of dialogue with Greek philosophy and reflection on the false paths offered by Arius finally to make clear the true path.

Likewise in ethical questions, as we have already noticed, it took time for Christian imagination to perceive that slavery was simply wrong. Similar accounts must be given of Christian perceptions of race and of women. I would argue that the equality of all races and the equality of the sexes are both implicit in Scripture, most evidently in the equal respect and regard that our Lord paid to all persons with whom he came in contact, Jew or gentile, man or woman, free or slave, and in the church's early realization that "in Christ" such distinctions ultimately could not and would not stand (Gal. 3.28; cf. Col. 3:11). But as David Brown has reminded us,[29] that all are valuable before God and will *ultimately* be equal does not necessarily imply present equality of ability, function, or status *now*. If it did, we should grant children the vote. If we are not ourselves to be blinded by our own current prejudices, we need to understand and accept that for many centuries vast numbers of well-meaning and intelligent men and women were persuaded, for a multitude of cultural and other reasons that necessarily appeared entirely valid to them, that there were inherent limitations and disabilities in women, or persons of another race, that made them incapable of equality in society with white males. It required complex historical processes leading to specific events, such as women doing so-called "men's work" perfectly effectively in World Wars I and II,[30] and African Americans flying fighter aircraft in combat with skill and courage in World War II,[31] to show us that these disabilities or limitations were in fact nonexistent or need not exist, and hence to bring home to us the true unacceptability of even benevolent forms of sexism or racism.

The exercise of imagination on our traditions leads us to new and deeper understandings of God and God's truth. Scripture, as we noted in our consideration of its differing voices and testimonies (testimonies and counter-testimonies) shows that this is the way in which God worked with our forebears, leading them to deeper understanding and sometimes revision of their traditions; and the history of the church since the closing of the canon shows that this continues to be the way God works with us. In the Bible God's word sometimes comes to those outside the people of God, as in God's call to the centurion Cornelius, which Cornelius then addresses to Peter (Acts 10). So later in the history of the church, as in the development of conscience that led to the abolition of slavery, there is often an interaction between the people of God and the world that goes in two directions. In this interaction, sometimes the people of God are behind the world in their perceptions, sometimes ahead of it, and sometimes needing simply to be reminded of what they already know, or ought to know.[32] The publication of Charles Darwin's *On the Origin of Species* (1859)[33] was, arguably, a good example of just such a reminder. Initially the Christian churches were appalled by Darwin's proposals.[34] Yet within thirty years the authors of *Lux Mundi* could manifest a deep and joyful creedal orthodoxy (thereby distinguishing themselves sharply from the authors of the earlier *Essays and Reviews*) and *at the same time* assume the propriety of evolutionary science and be willing to engage in conversation with it. In doing so, they saw themselves pointing to an "old almost forgotten truth of the immanence of the Word, the belief in God as 'creation's secret force'" This truth, far from being undermined, was "illumined and confirmed...by the advance of science," so that it now came to them "with all the power of new discovery."[35] As far as scriptural interpretation was concerned, I would argue that ceasing to regard Genesis 1 as a source of factual information actually freed its interpreters to see what it was really affirming, namely (as Walter Brueggemann puts it) a "serene governance" of the whole creation "from heaven"[36] (cf. Ps. 33, Proverbs 8, John 1:1-18).

This continuing back and forth between the people of God and the world, this bringing forth of things old and things new, is exactly as we should expect. Why should the

God who is self-revealing in these ways in Scripture suddenly cease to be the God who is self-revealing in these ways after the closure of the canon, so becoming in effect a God *other* than the God of Scripture? Or, as David Brown puts it, "It seems odd to postulate a God without revelatory impact upon the history of the Church when that history is not significantly different in fallibility and conditionedness from the history of the biblical community itself."[37]

To what areas of new reflection and understanding will Christian imagination be called in our day and in the decades immediately to come? To attempt to answer that is risky, of course: the Spirit blows where it wills. But I for one shall be surprised, first, if there are not such areas, for now as always the church is called to hand on the gospel. If the church is not a missionary church, that is, a "sent" (apostolic) church, then she is the church neither of Jesus Christ nor of the first witnesses to his resurrection, who were told not, "now you have been begotten to a living hope"—although they had, and would think about that later—but, "Go and tell!" And the church must carry out this mission in what will always in some ways be a new world, with new questions and new needs, or at least with its own versions of the old questions and the old needs. If the church is not listening and responding to these, as Saint Peter listened and responded to Cornelius (Acts 10:9 ff.), then it is in danger of making itself blind and deaf to the very situation into which the gospel is now to be translated. Here again, the exchange will be two-way, for the church in her turn will learn new dimensions of her faith from these new questions and new needs, just as Peter did from listening to Cornelius (Acts 10:34-35). As Bernard Sesboüé says, "the Gospel bears aspects which are still hidden, and which it is our duty to discover in the new today which God gives us."[38]

Secondly, I shall be surprised if these areas for new exercise of Christian imagination do not include those suggested by Sesboüé as "gospel tasks for today":[39] specifically, considering how proclamation of the gospel shall relate to the peculiar forms that unbelief takes in the twenty-first century; how we may continue to promote and enhance unity among Christians "that the world may believe"; how we may engage in interfaith dialogue in such a way as to remain faithful, witnessing with evangelical modesty to the gift we receive in Christ; and, finally, how the gospel relates to globalization, most notably to questions of international justice and politics.[40] And all this will require active imagination and theological reflection.

Of course, active imagination and theological reflection can make mistakes, and sometimes do. Hananiah the prophet made such a mistake (Jer. 28:1-17). So it seems—or very nearly!—did Saint Peter (Gal. 2:11-14). So did Marcion. So did Arius. So did those who formulated what Bart D. Ehrman has taught us to call "lost Christianities"[41]—not quite lost, of course, or Ehrman would not be able to write about them! Yes, mistakes can be made. But that is only to say what we have already said, that the history of the Church is and remains not significantly different from the history of the biblical community itself. And it is certainly not to be taken as a warning against theological reflection and imagination. On the contrary, it is from such things, even indirectly from the trial and then rejection of mistaken paths, that we learn new truths about our faith.

The fact that mistakes can be made is, however, a reminder of where the center is. The center is not whatever insight into doctrine or ethics we gain from theological reflection or imagination, however inspired or true those insights may be. Indeed, the center is not doctrine or ethics at all, for doctrine and ethics are not, essentially, what Christianity is about.

Doctrine is analysis of the Christian experience, the attempt to express that experience in concepts. Such analysis is, of course, precious. Ethics is our attempt to answer the question, "How, then, shall we live?" This process, too, is precious. But all these things follow from our *surrender to the story*. They must always be faith seeking understanding—*fides quaerens intellectum*—and the faith itself must first be directed to God, the God of the biblical story, the God who deals with Israel and is God-with-us in Jesus Christ, the same yesterday, today, and forever, the God who sends to us the light of the Holy Spirit: *that* God, however much and in whatever way our understanding may change or evolve.[42]

There is and must be a generic deficiency in doctrine, because rational reflection and argumentation, important and necessary as they are in certain circumstances, can never convey by themselves the realities of our relationship with God. One reason why the Scriptures are precious is the variety of their narrative. Their richness humbles us, exposing the weakness of our abstractions, which seem at first glance so much easier to grasp and more coherent than the biblical story, but which are in the long run so much thinner and less satisfying. Surely the Bible does not always answer our questions. But then, as Northrop Frye reminds us, "to answer a question is to consolidate the mental level on which the question is asked."[43] Rather, the Bible tends to keep something in reserve, suggesting that we may yet find better questions. The Bible has, indeed, a kind of reticence or shyness. And precisely through that, through being indirect and oblique, it is able to point at once to the way of affirmation (*via positiva*), "we have beheld his glory," *and* to the way of negation (*via negativa*), "now we see through a glass, darkly." So doing it brings home to us those great realities that *can* only be perceived by poetry and the imagination: "l'amor che move il sole e l'altre stelle." In its many voices, its contradictions, it might seem to be stammering; and indeed it is. But that is the point. How shall we *not* stammer, when we speak of the divine mystery?

Notes

1. Cf. Sir Edmund Hoskyns, "Christ of the Synoptic Gospels," in *Essays Catholic and Critical* (London: S.P.C.K., 1926), 151–78.
2. Cf. David Brown, *Tradition and Imagination* 107–108.
3. Cf. Steiner, *Real Presences*, 164–65 and passim.
4. See Valentine Cunningham, "Best Stories in the Best Order? Canons, Apocryphas, and (Post) Modern Reading," in *Literature and Theology* **14**.1 (2000), esp. 76–79.
5. In the next few paragraphs I make use of material I cited earlier in *A Preface to Romans: Notes on the Epistle in Its Literary and Social Setting* (New York: Oxford University Press, 2000), 50–54 (although to make a rather different point), and of arguments previously used in *And God Spoke: The Authority of the Bible for the Church Today* (Cambridge, Mass.: Cowley, 2002), 107–21.
6. Richard B. Hays, *The Moral Vision of the New Testament: A Contemporary Introduction to New Testament Ethics* (San Francisco: HarperSanFrancisco, 1996), 5–6.
7. Mark D. Nanos in *Review of Biblical Literature* at http://www.bookreviews.org/pdf/961_112.pdf, 2; cf. Bryan, *Preface to Romans*, 50–52.
8. Milman Parry, "The Historical Method in Literary Criticism," in *The Making of Homeric Verse: The Collected Papers of Milman Parry*, ed. Adam Parry (New York and Oxford: Oxford University Press, 1987), 408–13; reprinted from *HAB* **38** (1936): 778–82.
9. Parry, "Historical Method," 410–11 (779–80).
10. Charles Williams, *The Place of the Lion* (New York: Pellegrini & Cudahy, 1933).
11. See Marilyn Nelson, "Translator's Preface," in *Euripides, 1, Hecuba*, David R. Slavitt and Palmer Bovie, eds., (Philadelphia: University of Philadelphia Press, 1998) 73–75.

12. Marilyn Nelson's *Hecuba*; directed by David Landon; with Tarashai Lee as Hecuba (Tennessee Williams Center, Sewanee, February 23–26, 2011).

13. Paul Ricoeur, "Interpretative Narrative," David Pellauer, trans., in *The Book and the Text: The Bible and Literary Theory*, Regina Schwartz, ed. (Oxford: Basil Blackwell, 1990) 237.

14. Ricoeur, "Interpretative Narrative," 237.

15. Ricoeur, "Preface to Bultmann," 101–103.

16. Dorothy Sayers, *The Man Born to be King: A Play-Cycle on the Life of our Lord and Saviour Jesus Christ* (London: Victor Gollancz, 1943), 36–37.

17. Robert Alter, *The Art of Biblical Narrative* (New York: Basic Books, 1981).

18. Alter, *Art of Biblical Narrative*, 33.

19. *Qual è 'l geomètra che tutto s'affige*
per misurar lo cerchio, e non ritrova,
pensando, quel principio ond' elli indige,
    tal era io a quella vista nova:
veder voleva come si convenne
l'imago al cerchio e come vi s'indova;
    ma non eran da ciò le proprie penne:
se non che la mia mente fu percossa
da un fulgore in che sua voglia venne.
    A l'alta fantasia qui mancò possa;
ma già volgeva il mio disio e 'l velle,
sì come rota ch'igualmente è mossa,
    l'amor che move il sole e l'altre stelle. (Dante Alighieri, Paradiso 33.133–45)

20. Ong, *Interfaces* 262, 263. Ong appears to me to have stated this quality of the Scriptural narrative admirably: my only respectful disagreement is that (as I have tried to show above) the New Testament is not utterly unique in this characteristic, though I grant it is unique in the force and power with which it expresses it. It may also be significant that, so far as I can see, all the examples of such "story that is not finished, nor is it meant to be" that I have cited are Christian.

21. On Mark 16:1-8, which is frequently misunderstood, see Bryan, Resurrection of the Messiah, 75–81.

22. "Commèdia," *Lo Zingarelli 1994: Vocabolario della lingua italiana*, Miro Dogliotti and Luigi Rosiello, eds. 12th edit. (Bologna: Zanichelli, 1993), 404.

23. See Matthew Levering, *Participatory Biblical Exegesis: A Theology of Biblical Interpretation* (Notre Dame, Ind.: University of Notre Dame Press, 2008), passim.

24. Umberto Eco and Cardinal Carlo Maria Martini, *Belief or Nonbelief: A Confrontation*, Minna Proctor, transl. (New York: Arcade, 1997), 32.

25. C. S. Lewis, *Miracles: A Preliminary Study* (London: Geoffrey Bles, 1947; revised 1960) Ch. 15, note 1.

26. Ibid.

27. Auerbach, 16.

28. Auerbach, 14–15.

29. *Discipleship and Imagination*, 30.

30. Carol Harris, *Women at War: The Home Front 1939-1945* (Stroud: Sutton Publishing, 2000) and *Women at War in Uniform 1939-1945* (Stroud: Sutton Publishing, 2002), passim.

31. Lynn M. Homan and Thomas Reilly. *Black Knights: The Story of the Tuskegee Airmen* (Gretna, La.: Pelican, 2001) 81–83, 116 and passim.

32. See Sesboüé, *Gospel and Tradition*, 157–62.

33. Charles Darwin, *On the Origin of Species by Means of Natural Selection, or the Preservation of Favoured Races in the Struggle for Life* (London: John Murray, 1859). For the 6th edition (1872), the title was changed to *The Origin of Species*.

34. See *Charles Darwin and the Tree of Life* and *Darwin's Struggle— The Evolution of the Origin of Species* (DVD: BBC Earth, 2009). My only criticism of these surveys is that Christian unreadiness to deal with Darwin's proposals is repeatedly described in them as "Anglican." In fact *no* major Christian denomination, Reformed or Roman Catholic, was ready to deal with Darwin. When serious dialogue did begin, the Anglican *Lux Mundi* (see above and n. 35) was, as it happened, among the earliest to engage in it from the Christian side.

35. Aubrey Moore, "The Christian Doctrine of God" in *Lux Mundi: A Series of Studies on the Religion of the Incarnation*, Charles Gore, ed. 10th edition (London: John Murray, 1891) 75–76; cf. Gore's own remarks on the purpose of *Lux Mundi* in his "Preface to the Tenth Edition," x-xi. Of course there continue to be those on both sides of the "religion versus anti-religion" divide who insist, virtually without debate, that theism and evolutionary hypotheses are incompatible, as in Richard A. Dawkins, *The God Delusion* (Boston: Houghton Mifflin, 2006) passim; but there are also many who carry on the discussion in an informed and rational manner: cf. e.g. (from the theological side) Cynthia Crysdale and Neil Ormerod, *Creator God, Evolving World* (Minneapolis: Fortress, 2013), and from the scientific, Arnold Benz, *The Future of the Universe: Chance, Chaos, God?* (New York: Continuum, 2000) (Benz is an astrophysicist) and David George Haskell, *The Forest Unseen: A Year's Watch in Nature* (New York: Viking, 2012) (Haskell is a biologist). On the (erroneous) assumption, still made by many (including Dawkins), that there is a necessary contradiction between the notion of divine providence or design in the world's affairs and the notion of freedom or chance, see Neil Ormerod, "Questions in Understanding Divine Action," in *Sewanee Theological Review* 56.4 (2013) 337–46.
36. Walter Brueggemann, *Old Testament Theology* (Minneapolis: Fortress, 1997) 154; cf. 344–45.
37. Brown, *Tradition and Imagination: Revelation and Change* 5.
38. Sesboüé, *Gospel and Tradition*, 175.
39. Sesboüé, *Gospel and Tradition*, 181.
40. Sesboüé, *Gospel and Tradition*, 181–87.
41. Bart D. Ehrman, *The Lost Christianities: The Battles for Scripture and the Faiths We Never Knew* (New York: Oxford University Press, 2003); see also, and seminally, Helmut Koester, "Gnomai Diaphorai" in James M. Robinson and Helmut Koester, *Trajectories Through Early Christianity* (Philadelphia: Fortress, 1971), 114–57.
42. Cf. Bryan, *Preface to Mark*, 166–67; C. S. Lewis, "The Language of Religion" in *C. S. Lewis: Essay Collection and Other Short Pieces*, ed. Lesley Walmsley (London: HarperCollins, 2000) 261.
43. Frye, *The Great Code* xv.

X

THE DRAMA OF THE WORD

Blessed Lord, who hast caused all Holy Scriptures to be written for our learning: Grant that we may in such wise hear them, read, mark, learn, and inwardly digest them,[1] that by patience, and comfort of thy holy Word, we may embrace, and ever hold fast the blessed hope of everlasting life, which thou hast given us in our Saviour Jesus Christ, who liveth and reigneth with thee and the Holy Spirit, one God, for ever and ever. Amen.

I WISH NOW TO TURN to a mode of biblical interpretation that I have so far ignored: and the fact that I have ignored it, and that those who read what I have written may not even have noticed, is evidence of how far we both are from the culture and custom that produced these texts. For our forebears in antiquity took it for granted that most people would experience most words, including sacred words, by hearing them. When someone first pointed that out to me, I immediately thought, "Well, so what? That was bound to be so when there was no printing and most people couldn't read." But I was wrong—or, at least, I was vastly oversimplifying—for the ancient view of words was shaped by far more than a mere lack of technology. As the collect that I have just quoted in its seventeenth century form[2] implies, well after the invention of printing, those who thought seriously about language still thought of it as sound, "as breath cast into the air."[3] Written texts, including printed texts, were essentially *a preparation for utterance.*

We may be quite sure that the early Christians shared this understanding of language. When the New Testament texts were collected and recognized as sacred, their role within the communities that assembled them was already established: they were performed, and such performance was understood to affect the ethos of both performer and community. In the early church, as William Shiell says, "Christian performances are about not only a saving event but also a saving person who said, 'This do in remembrance of me.' As the texts are performed, they are remembering the person and the people who have become part of the living conversation within the performance."[4]

Havelock Ellis, Walter Ong, and others have pointed out what an enormous difference writing of any kind, either by hand ("chirographic") or by printing ("typographic"), makes. It is a simple matter of fact that the origins of language are aural and oral. We learn by hearing, initially from our first caregivers (hence we speak of our "mother tongue"), and afterward from everyone around us. As Maryanne Wolf has shown us, "in the evolution of our brain's capacity to learn, the act of reading is not natural." The fact that we can do it at all is evidence of the brain's marvelous adaptability.[5]

Walter Ong draws our attention to the degree to which human experience of alienation may be linked to the invention of writing. Put briefly, the world of primary orality is integrative, communal, and integrating. The elements of its discourse tend to be formulaic. They are familiar to those who use them—*A stitch in time saves nine, Too many cooks spoil the broth*—and so they bind those who know to what they know in ways that are comfortable because they are familiar. The world of writing, by contrast, is detached and distancing. This is not to claim that writing or printing is bad for humanity. Quite the contrary! Sometimes—as when we wish to think clearly about the nature of something, or to analyze a situation—the distancing that is afforded by "media" is valuable and necessary. A friend of mine, a professional photographer, used to say that he photographed things because by doing so he found out how he felt about them. Many of us, surely, have had the experience of clarifying our thoughts by putting them into written form. Plato, notoriously, wanted to exclude poets from his republic: which is to say, he wanted to exclude *oral* poets such as Homer, and that was because the kind of knowledge they conferred—oral, holistic, formulaic—was not compatible with the kind of clear thinking and analysis that he wanted.

Orality, then, is communal, and bonding. Whether that bonding is good or bad, healthy or unhealthy, depends on many things, including the nature of the oral message. That was something very well understood by the ancient writers on rhetoric. Quintilian said that if you are truly to be a good speaker—good in every sense of the word—then *you must also be a good person* (*Inst. Or.* 12.1.1-3). Twelve or so centuries later, Desiderius Erasmus was encouraging studies by which young men would learn "the power of honesty and the nature of probity, which are the especial virtues of eloquence."[6] In other words, there was a connection between your quality as a speaker and your quality as a person. Your *ethos* mattered. Clearly Quintilian and Erasmus made a distinction between rhetoric that was merely effective in working the speaker's will on the crowd and a rhetoric that was *both* effective *and* healthy.

This whole subject of the relationship of orality to written text is a fascinating one, now further complicated by the growth of electronic media, and this is not the place to pursue it. Those who are interested will turn to the work of Milman Parry, Albert B. Lord, Havelock Ellis, and Walter Ong. I would also want to argue for a direct relationship between the growing dominance since the Enlightenment of written texts over spoken word and, during the same period, the development for good and ill of the phenomenon of individualism.[7] Though valuable in its emphases on human rights and responsibilities, individualism in its extreme forms can be destructive—as, for example, in the United States' apparent inability (as I write in 2012) to create for itself decent national health care or a rational system of gun control. Here, alas, is a perfect illustration of the dictum that good things made into idols become demons.

For my immediate purposes, however, as regards the study and interpretation of Scripture, I simply want to focus on one key difference between the oral and written word. The written word tends by its very nature to be disjunctive, separating the utterer from the audience, so that we sometimes speak even of a living person's writing as their "testament" or "memorial"—as if they were already dead. And, of course, one *advantage* of the written over the spoken word is that it can continue to "memorialize" an author even after that person really has died. In this way Virgil and Dante still speak to us. The *merely* spoken word is, by contrast, entirely time-bound. So we might observe that among the nations and empires of the ancient world, the Israelites did not achieve much. It was pagans who forged mighty empires, won great battles, and built the most magnificent pyramids, palaces, and temples. Even Israel's temple at Jerusalem, which the Chronicler thought wonderful, seems by many ancient standards to have been a quite modest affair. What the Israelites did do, however, was to produce a book, and their book lives on. Through it, they continue to address and influence the world.[8]

The *disadvantage* of the written word is that by the very fact of being written it loses the quality of shared life that is characteristic of living words exchanged. Ong expresses the matter with his usual clarity:

> The spoken word, however abstract its signification or however static the object it may represent, is of its very nature a sound, tied to the movement of life itself in the flow of time. Sound exists only when it is going out of existence: in uttering the word "existence," by the time I get to the "-tence," the "exist-" is gone and has to be gone…No real word can be present all at once as the letters in a written "word" are. The real word, the spoken word, is always an event, whatever its codified associations with concepts, thought of as immobile objectifications. In this sense the spoken word is an action, an ongoing part of ongoing existence.

Oral utterance thus encourages a sense of continuity with life, a sense of participation, because it is itself participatory. Writing and print, despite their intrinsic value, obscure the nature of the word and of thought itself, for they sequester the essentially participatory word—fruitfully enough, beyond a doubt—from its natural habitat, which is sound, and assimilate it to a mark on a surface, where a real word cannot exist at all.

This is the problem of written text. But it is also the opportunity for performers: for by allowing written words to be again "formed through" them (which is essentially what "performance" means), performers can restore to past words some—perhaps all—of that participatory quality which is natural to words in their original oral state, and which being confined to writing denies them. Words from the past, which have been bereft of much of their power through disembodiment, are re-embodied, made incarnate, through the person of the performer. And that re-embodiment can enable those words to live again and involve us as much as if we were now hearing them for the first time, or even as if they were being said for the first time. Every actor worth his or her salt knows this, and every actor worth his or her salt seeks to achieve it in performance.

What, then, of the reading aloud of Scripture in the liturgy? Evidently, the primary task of one who reads Scripture in the liturgy is to return these words to their native element, so that they are no longer just marks on a page but event, deed, action, a "drama of the word"—the Greek word *drama* means, essentially, action or deed, and only comes by use to mean the representation of such action on the stage. But of performance (the deliberate delivery of a text in public for an audience) as opposed to, say, conversation, we must say more. "Language fully owned ... has the power to transform. There is a summoning power in words: it is sometimes dangerous to say what we mean because it will occur. Powerful words and ideas create the thing itself. Ask with clarity and passion, and you will receive."[9] So Patsy Rodenburg, widely recognized as among the world's leading voice and drama coaches: and in expecting such a summoning power of the spoken word in our delivery of Scripture, we are, as we began by noting, in one way nearer to the original texts and their intention than any purely private and personal study of them can ever be. For this is how they were used from the beginning, and this is how their authors expected them to be used.

Evidently, for the lector, this presents an opportunity, a challenge, and a serious responsibility. It is not a matter of being "theatrical" (in a bad sense). There is an appropriate way to communicate in one situation and an appropriate way in another. One does not address a group of retired professionals as one would a group of seven-year-olds, and one does not deliver a text at the Holy Eucharist as one would deliver it onstage at the Old Vic. And bad acting is bad acting in any situation. But there are certain principles that apply to all good delivery. We sometimes speak of an effective speaker or performer as having "presence," and such "presence" is, no doubt, a gift. It is, however, a gift honed and made effective by craft.

For modern English speakers such craft includes an awareness of English prosody, that is to say (and as etymology indicates) the *music* of speech[10]—what David Landon calls "the music of thought."[11] These involve techniques of stress, rhythm, and pitch that most of us use naturally in conversation[12] yet must *learn* to use when reading aloud from a text—presumably because, as we have noted, reading texts is in itself not natural to us. Along with this must go an understanding of the chosen reading, a view of why whoever speaks says what they say, and above all a commitment to say all that we say with intention, for only when we speak with intention do we speak effectively. Patsy Rodenburg goes so far as to say, "Understanding the word is not enough—you should have an experience of it."[13] Serious performers must be willing, in the deepest sense of which they are capable, to "know" the text and sit under its judgment. "Be it unto me according to thy word" is a necessary commitment for them, as is "dying to self." It is not my purpose here to discuss these techniques and commitments, although they are important.[14]

My purpose is to take note of them, and to emphasize that by means of them readers become in their own way interpreters of Scripture: for when we speak a text effectively so that it grasps an audience, we are not simply saying the words aloud, we are interpreting them. That is why we speak of this or that actor's interpretation of Rosalind or Hamlet.

What is the value of this kind of interpretation? How does it relate to the kinds of interpretation that I have been discussing in the previous chapters of this book? George Steiner in *Real Presences* offers a "parable or rational fiction" of a society where all secondary literature—literary reviews, talk about the arts, and books about books would be forbidden. There would only be those who made art, and those who responded to it.[15] Does that mean Steiner advocates a blank and passive silence around the creative imagination? Does it mean there would be no appreciation, no interpretation, no hermeneutic? Not at all! For in Steiner's view the true interpreters of art are not reviewers, critics, or academic experts at all, but those who perform it.

> Each performance of a dramatic text or musical score is a critique in the most vital sense of the term: it is an act of penetrative response which makes sense sensible. The 'dramatic critic' *par excellence* is the actor and the producer who, with and through the actor, tests and carries out the potentialities of meaning in the play.[16]

There is, moreover, as Steiner points out, a moral aspect to this. Performers put themselves on the line. They take the risk of being out there, of being counted. Unlike mere reviewers or literary critics, performers invest their own beings in the process of their interpretations. Their readings, their enactments of chosen meanings and values, "are not those of external survey. They are a commitment, a response which is, in the root sense, responsible."[17]

Of course, and as Steiner genially admits in the next chapter, his little parable is a hyperbole. There *is* a place for secondary criticism and review, and the best of it amounts to creative writing in its own right—he instances Eric Auerbach's *Mimesis*, and so would I. I would also instance Steiner's own work. Still, Steiner's fiction does sharpen the question that I posed at the beginning of my previous paragraph: what then *is* the proper relationship between performance and secondary literature, the academic work of library and study, and the drama of the word?

We may safely begin by saying that the secondary literature is at least, or ought to be, a resource. A good actor does not undertake a role in an Elizabethan drama without learning what can be learned of Elizabethan theater, Elizabethan vocabulary and idiom, and the peculiar workings of Elizabethan dramatic verse. In the same way, the good performer of Scripture will want to make use of whatever historical- and literary-critical tools are available. I have just finished working with a group of young actors who, with breathtaking effect, gave a dramatic rendering of the Passion according to Saint Mark in All Saints' Chapel, Sewanee, on Palm Sunday, 2012. In preparation for their performance, an important part was played by reflection on just such insights as the scholar's study has to offer: on the foundation of the passion narrative on the four pillars of the apostolic gospel as outlined by Paul—that Christ died, he was buried, he has been raised, and he appeared (1 Cor. 15:3-5);[18] on the uniqueness of such a narrative as that of Peter's denial in the literature of the ancient world, in that it takes with tragic

seriousness the spiritual struggles of an ordinary, working man; on the shamefulness of Pilate's part in the action;
on the irony of the cohort's "legionary salute" to Jesus, and
of the salutes offered by others to Jesus as he hangs on the
cross; on the significance of the named eyewitnesses, who
must have been known to Mark's first hearers; on the significance of the rending of the Temple veil; on the significance
of the Centurion's words; on the role of Joseph of Arimathea,
a member of the very Sanhedrin that had condemned Jesus.
All these were legitimate matters for reflection and guidance
as the actors sought to place themselves under the text and
make their interpretative choices in performing it.

It will be noted, however, that the historical critical questions on which the actors found themselves reflecting were
all questions directly involving *the text*—its intention, its
meaning, and its significance: and this focus suggests how
performance may indeed not only draw on but also feed back
into other forms of review and interpretation, offering cor-
rective and direction. For the strength of performative interpretation is that it is by its nature tied to its primary source,
and so has some built-in protection from the temptation to
deviate from it. I say "some," for of course even here the protection is not complete: performances may be designed not
to perform the text but to perform against it, as in those pre-
sentations of *Hamlet* and *Don Giovanni* that we noticed earlier.[19] Still, temptation to turn away from the primary source
is far more prevalent in the academic world, where allegedly
interpretative discourse regularly succumbs to it. Steiner's
description of much that we do is, alas, only too near to the
truth: "Monograph feeds on monograph, vision on revision.
The primary text is only the remote font of autonomous exe-
getic proliferation."[20]

In our earlier reflections we have observed that we can never truly encounter a text unless we make some effort to go where that text intends to take us, to understand and interpret it on its own terms: with Shakespeare we must go to the theater, with Jane Austen we must read her novels as novels. By that process, and that alone, we shall discover whether the encounter is worthwhile. It is no different with Scripture. Scripture's *sitz im leben* is being heard, in synagogue and church. Unless, then, we are prepared to be serious about that—and therefore about performance, which is its necessary condition—we can claim to be no more than partially serious in our desire to encounter Scripture, or to discover whether that encounter is worthwhile.

Where, then, should one start? The effect achieved by our young actors was, as I have said, breathtaking—and a far cry indeed from that experience of "someone reading the lesson," which is only too common in our worship: the desultory recital of words in front of a group that hears nothing to any purpose, being therefore understandably and legitimately bored with the whole thing. Of course not every church on every Sunday can call upon a group of willing, thoughtful, and talented young actors. Nevertheless, between the richness of the one and mere poverty there is a range of possibilities. In many churches, faithful members of the choir do the best they can with the music each Sunday, and we honor them for it. Is it too much to ask that the appointed lections be entrusted to faithful members of the congregation, chosen because they may actually have some gift for this particular form of interpretation and are willing to take the risks involved in putting it out there? Can we not find lectors who are willing to take the same care over their readings as members of the choir do over their music?

Notes

1. See Ong, *Interfaces of the Word*, 24.
2. *The Book of Common Prayer* 1662, Collect for the Second Sunday in Advent. This collect was composed for the 1549 Book of Common Prayer.
3. Jonathan Hope, *Shakespeare Language: Reason, Eloquence and Artifice in the Renaissance*, Arden Shakespeare (London: Methuen Drama A. & C. Black, 2010), 40; and passim.
4. William D. Shiell, *Delivering from Memory: The Effect of Performance on the Early Christian Audience* (Eugene, Ore: Pickwick Publications, 2011), 104.
5. Maryanne Wolf, *Proust and the Squid* (New York: HarperCollins, 2007), 8, and passim.
6. Cited in T. W. Baldwin, *William Shakespeare's Small Latine and Lesse Greek* (University of Illinois, 1944) 2.241, who cites Erasmus, *Opera* (1703) 352–54.
7. See Christopher Bryan, "Individualism" in *STR* **41**.1 (1997): 3–9 and (to redress a balance that I may have tipped too far) Marilynne Robinson's beautiful essay, "When I was a child" in *When I Was a Child I Read Books* (New York: Farrar, Straus, and Giroux, 2012) 85–94.
8. See Frye, *The Great Code* ref.
9. Patsy Rodenburg, *Speaking Shakespeare* (London and New York: Palgrave Macmillan, 2002), 193.
10. I.e.. πρός to (also toward, close to, approaching to, in addition) + ᾠδή song (*OED2*, "prosody").
11. Additional Note A: David Landon, "Speaking the Word: a Guide to Liturgical Reading" 133–58.
12. There are, alas, exceptions: prosody is a function of the right side of the brain, and people with right-brain lesions tend to speak in a "flattened tone of voice and a lack of emotional expression: they lack prosody." They also have trouble picking up the "musical cues" in what others say, the notes of irony, enthusiasm, questioning, and so on: see Michael R. Trimble, *The Soul in the Brain: The Cerebral Basis of Language, Art, and Belief* (Johns Hopkins, 2007), 69.

13. Patsy Rodenburg, *Speaking Shakespeare* (London and New York: Palgrave Macmillan, 2002), 355. See further Additional Note A: David Landon, "Speaking the Word" 133–58.
14. But see Additional Note A: David Landon, "Speaking the Word" 133–58.
15. George Steiner, *Real Presences* (London: Faber and Faber / Chicago: University of Chicago, 1989), 4ff.
16. Steiner, *Real Presences*, 8.
17. Steiner, *Real Presences*, 8.
18. See further Bryan, *Resurrection of the Messiah*, 69 and passim.
19. See above, p. 000.
20. Steiner, *Real Presences* 39.

EPILOGUE

In my consideration of both secondary literature and performance, I have been advocating an approach to biblical interpretation, which is what Matthew Levering, if I understand
him correctly, advocates as "participatory exegesis"[1]—exegesis consciously and unapologetically carried on within
the fellowship of the Church and, more importantly, of the
Triune God and the resurrected Christ. This does not mean
that biblical interpretation may ignore the specificity of scientific questions, or force its results into conformity with a
set of ecclesial propositions. Honest questions honestly asked
retain their autonomy and their integrity. It does mean that
in asking those questions of the texts we shall not ignore the
texts' setting-in-life (*sitz im leben*), which is indeed (as it is
for all things) an element in what they are. It may well be
claimed that in thus insisting on scholarly examination of
the Scriptures, but always in the context of the reader's own
faith and formation, I am saying nothing new. And indeed
I am not. The Victorines in the twelfth century had just such

a model.[2] But perhaps it is at least something that may profitably be *re*newed at the present time.

Participatory interpretation means that when we have carried out our historical- and literary-critical work to the best of our ability, we must then consider the problem that Damaris Tighe refused to consider: "How might what this text says bear on my life?" Performance in particular, by re-embodying the texts, tends to force these questions upon us; but there is no reason why even in the study and the library we may not go on from historical analysis to ask the three further questions associated with exegesis in former ages: what do our texts tell us about our *faith* now? (their "allegorical" sense); what do they tell us about how we should *act* now? (their "moral" sense); and what do they tell us about what we should *hope* for (their "anagogical" sense).[3]

Theologians of the Reformation used to speak of the Scriptures as possessing "clarity" or "transparency" (*perspicuitas*), by which they did not mean they were easy to understand, but that the effort to understand them, if made honestly and faithfully, would always, in the end, bear good fruit. No doubt in saying this some Reformers were driven by a desire to lessen the significance of, or even remove the necessity for, a teaching office of the church; and some seemed to forget that even on the plane of humanly observable history the canon of Holy Scripture was evidently formed not independently of the church but in and as a part of its life—its worship, its ministry, and its faith. Nevertheless, the Reformers' view was essentially correct. Where the Scriptures are read in the fellowship of faith, under the guidance of the living voice of the Church, her Creeds, and her Sacraments, this *perspicuitas*, this transparency to Christ, *is* a work of the Holy Spirit through them.

Which leads us to the last thing that needs to be said, which though last, is by no means of least importance. I have spoken of the careful attention and deep reading that is required for interpretation and performance of any text: but of course from a Christian point of view the Bible is not just any text, nor even any great text. It is a creation of the Holy Spirit (cf. 2 Peter 1.21), and therefore its proper interpretation can only be through the Spirit (1 Cor. 2:9-16).

No doubt mere intelligence and hard work will give us some understanding of these texts. Indeed, these will be necessary. No one could deny that the enterprise I have described in the foregoing chapters is formidable. No one who undertakes it can expect to succeed without diligence and hard work. There must be, as renaissance students of human nature would have put it, *decoro*—decorum: which is to say, the subject must be treated properly, given its due.

Yet those who interpret in the fellowship of the church will not take even their own diligence with complete gravity. They will relish the uncertainty, the risk that goes with any human enterprise. In other words, they will try to cultivate a second quality that those renaissance students of human nature would have called *sprezzatura*—sometimes translated "nonchalance": a relaxed joy in things that, while it will allow us, even encourage us, to do whatever our hand finds to do with all our might, will yet discourage us from overestimating the significance of what we do. In its negative sense, sprezzatura means "contempt." Positively, it speaks of modesty: a refusal to take oneself or one's works too seriously, as if God might be dethroned without them. It is a quality that was encouraged in us by Father Crisp, my parish priest when I was a boy. Over a complex liturgy or sermon, he would smile and say, "We do the best we can to make it as good as we can—but then, when it comes time for it, and even if it goes haywire, we just *offer it up!*" It's a quality that has marked the greatest theologians, from Thomas speaking of his work as "straw" in comparison with the glory to which it bore witness, to Karl Barth picturing how the angels must laugh at him: "There he goes with his wheelbarrow full of books on dogmatics!"

To cultivate sprezzatura is to concede that even our best efforts, if they are to be worth anything at all, need a gift—a *third* quality that cannot be controlled or cultivated at all, but only prayed for. That quality, that gift, is what the renaissance students referred to as *grazia*, grace. Surely one reason why God calls very flawed and sinful persons to priesthood, and why such flawed and sinful persons, uttering words about and presuming to act in the name of a God Whom they scarcely at all understand and certainly do not serve very well, are yet occasionally used as instruments of God's purposes, is precisely to show that God can take hold of and work through a very flawed and sinful life: which is to say, anyone's life.[4] When this happens (as on occasion even Saint Paul had to be reminded), what is being manifested is *grazia*, Christ's grace, the gift of God, which is "sufficient" for us, whereby God's power is made perfect precisely by way of our weakness (2 Cor. 12.9-10; cf. 2 Cor. 4.7).

Those who would interpret biblical texts in the service of the church should know that they need the support and guidance of the Holy Spirit, whether that leads to adoration, confession, or action, to writing commentaries or preaching sermons or performing texts, to visiting the sick or standing up for human rights. As Enzo Bianchi puts it,

> The human heart was made for the Word and the Word for the heart. The lyrics of Psalm 119:111 describe this marriage, in which God's Word becomes your own and your heart sings out the joy of belonging to God. This is the heart of a disciple, a heart so receptive to God's intentions that it can experience the Word with little or no explanation, a heart truly seated at Christ's feet and ready to listen like Mary of Bethany (Lk 10:39), a heart capable of storing the biblical words and reflecting on them as Mary the Mother of Jesus did (Lk 2:19 and 51). This kind of heart can be yours.[5]

Notes

1. Levering, *Participatory Biblical Exegesis*, passim; cf. Adrian Walker, "Fundamentalism and the Catholicity of Truth," in *Communio* **29** (2002): 21; cf. Dale B. Martin, *Pedagogy of the Bible: An Analysis and Proposal* (Louisville, Ky.: Westminster John Knox, 2008), 97–109; Daniel J. Harrington, S. J., "Reading the Bible Critically and Religiously," and Peter Enns's "Response," in Marc Zvi Brettler, Peter Enns, and Daniel Harrington, S. J., *The Bible and the Believer: How to Read the Bible Critically and Religiously* (Oxford: Oxford University Press, 2012), 80–118.
2. See *Victorine Texts in Translation: Exegesis, Theology and Spirituality from the Abbey of St Victor, 3, Interpretation of Scripture: Theory*, Franklin T. Harkins and Frans van Liere, eds. (Turnhout, Belgium: Brepols, 2012), 31–36, although the entire volume could stand as an illustration of my claim.
3. See Bryan, *And God Spoke*, 98–104; and for full discussion, Henri de Lubac, *Medieval Exegesis, 1, The Four Senses of Scripture*, Mark Sebank, transl. (Grand Rapids, Mich.: William B. Eerdmans / Edinburgh: T. & T. Clark, 1998 [1959]).

4. See John E. Keegan, "Reflections on the Priesthood after Reading Julia Gatta's *The Nearness of God*," in *STR* *55*.4 (2012): 405; cf. Julia Gatta, *The Nearness of God* (New York: Morehouse, 2010).
5. Enzo Bianchi, *Praying the Word: An Introduction to Lectio Divina*, James W. Zona, transl. (Kalamazoo, Mich.: Cistercian Publications, 1998), 90–91.

APPENDIX

SPEAKING THE WORD: A GUIDE TO

LITURGICAL READING

BY DAVID LANDON

There is an art to reading Scripture in the liturgy: the art of returning the word on the page to the world of spoken discourse, what Walter Ong—echoing Martin Buber—calls the "I-Thou world."[1] Ong, throughout his long career as a scholar and critic, sought to remind our print-bound culture of what he called the "primacy of the oral." Literature, Ong suggests, is a form of speech; it is as instinctive to our being as our need for breath, or a child's cry.

> To consider the work of literature in its primary oral and aural existence, we must enter profoundly into this world of sound as such, the I-Thou world where, through the mysterious interior resonance which sound best of all provides, persons commune with persons... All verbalization, including literature, is radically a cry, a sound emitted from the interior of a person, a modification of one's exhalation of breath which contains the

> intimate connection with life which we find in breath itself, and which registers in the etymology of the word "spirit," that is breath.[1]

But if this is so, and if Scripture—as Christopher Bryan has argued—is a form of literature, why do we need an art of communicating scripture orally? Why can't we just read scripture "naturally?" Because, I would suggest on the basis of my experience as a teacher, most of us do not do it "naturally" at all. We tend either to read scripture in some habitual, half-schooled way, without thought, inflection, or feeling, or we seek to read it authoritatively, delivering the "lesson" from the elevation of the lectern. Some argue this is preferable to the dangers of dramatic interpretation, cautioning us against intruding on sacred text. But to deliver the words of scripture impersonally, as if they were so many inert facts on the page, is to deny the nature of those words as utterance, robbing them of breath and spirit. To speak scripture "naturally," we have to do it artfully, with very close attention and sensitivity to the text.

The art of speaking text has a distinguished history. *Pronunciatio,* reading out loud, was one of the foundational practices of a classical education. It was the first step in the acquisition of rhetorical skill, the ability to deliver a tightly composed text as if the speaker were discovering what needed to be said in the moment, extempore. Classical rhetoric has been associated with the Christian tradition since the beginning. We need only think of the epistles of Saint Paul, or Saint Augustine's immensely influential *On Christian Learning* to realize that the church has always valued eloquence.[2] During the English Reformation, in Elizabethan and Jacobean grammar schools, young scholars—such as

George Herbert at Westminster School, Lancelot Andrewes at the Merchant Taylors' School, or Richard Hooker and William Shakespeare at the Exeter and Stratford Grammar Schools, respectively—would have been called on every day to read out loud from the great Latin authors. They would each have been instructed to read:

- "Not as a boy who is saying his lesson," but as if "feigning to speak," that is: as if he were an "I" speaking to a "thou."
- "With pleasing and apt modulation, tempered with variety" so as to make the thought "manifest."
- "Audibly, leisurely, distinctly, and naturally, sounding out especially the last syllable, that each word may be understood."
- "Diversely, according to the variety of passions that are to be expressed."
- "Pathetically," or as we would say, "with empathy."
- "With judgment," observing "his commas, colons, and full points, his parentheses, his breathing spaces, and distinctions."[3]

This is excellent and expert advice, of course, but how do we go about putting it into practice? How do we return anything so deliberate as written text to the spontaneity and musicality of speech?[4] We will go about it deliberately by a method known as layering: by isolating the various elements of speech and working on them one lesson at a time. Our goal is to put all the elements together: to say our lesson not as a schoolboy repeating his lesson, but "naturally," as if "feigning to speak." This takes patience. But the process is a little like learning to ride a bicycle, or to swim. With practice, we get the feel of it and just go.

As our practice text we will use Paul's hymn to love at 1 Corinthians 13, a text widely recognized for its rhetorical power and beauty.[5] The passage falls into three rhetorical periods, or sections, each with its particular momentum and music. The first section sets up the proposition: "without love we are nothing." The second section defines love. The third section contrasts the imperfection of the transient "now" with the perfect fulfillment of the "love that never ends," and concludes with a reaffirmation of love.

Here is the whole passage:

1) If I speak in the tongues of men and of angels, but have not love, I am a noisy gong or a clanging cymbal. And if I have prophetic powers, and understand all mysteries and all knowledge, and if I have all faith, so as to remove mountains, but have not love, I am nothing. If I give away all I have, and if I deliver my body to be burned, but have not love, I gain nothing.

2) Love is patient and kind; love is not jealous or boastful; it is not arrogant or rude. Love does not insist on its own way; it is not irritable or resentful; it does not rejoice at wrong, but rejoices in the right. Love bears all things, believes all things, hopes all things, endures all things. Love never ends;

3) as for prophecies, they will pass away; as for tongues, they will cease; as for knowledge, it will pass away. For our knowledge is imperfect and our prophecy is imperfect; but when the perfect comes, the imperfect will pass away. When I was a child, I spoke like a child, I thought like a child, I reasoned like a child; when I became a man, I gave up childish ways. For now we see in a mirror dimly, but then face to face.

Now I know in part; then I shall understand fully, even as I have been fully understood. So faith, hope, love abide, these three; but the greatest of these is love.

Lesson One: Intonation Groups. We do not naturally think in sentences. Our thought moves in relatively short phrases of three or four words, lasting only about one or two seconds. These phrases may or may not be separated by punctuation. A millisecond thought shift (perhaps even a slight pause) distinguishes each phrase from the phrase that follows. The neurolinguist Wallace Chafe calls these phrases "intonation groups" because we instinctively use pitch to separate one group from another, generally lifting the pitch to indicate the thought is continuing, lowering the pitch to indicate the thought is concluding.[6] Here, then, is the first movement of 1 Corinthians 13, arranged according to intonation groups:

If I *speak* /
   in the tongues of *men* /
   and of *angels,* /
but have not *love,* /
I am a noisy *gong* /
   or a clanging *cymbal.* /
And if I have prophetic *powers,* /
and understand all *mysteries* /
   and all *knowledge,* /
and if I have all *faith,* /
so as to remove *mountains,* /
but have not *love,* /
I am *nothing.* /
If I give *away* /

all I *have* /
and If I *deliver* /
my body to be *burned* /
but have not *love* /
I gain *nothing.*

EXERCISES FOR INTONATION:

- Read the passage out loud. Lift the pitch slightly on the italicized words when the thought is continuing. Drop the pitch when the thought concludes, as on *cymbal* and *nothing.*
- Try tapping your foot as you speak the italicized words.
- Distinctions in pitch help make the thought "manifest." Try varying the pitch of the last words of the intonation groups.
- If you are adventurous, try walking the words. Give a little stamp as you speak the word at the end of each group. Shift direction as you say the first word of the next group.
- Do this deliberately at first, but as you get the feel of the exercise, allow your body to respond to the momentum of the text. Find "the dance of the words." For instance, you can give a little jump on the last word. Or make a gesture. Pirouette as you shift direction. Hop on one foot as you speak the phrase, switch to the other for the last word in the phrase.
- Notice how the phrases tend to build toward the last word in the group, generally the important word in the group.

- Try singing the last word of the phrase as you continue to move about.
- Invent your own exercise.[7]

Table 12.1

About Intonation. Intonation groups can vary from speaker to speaker. For instance, one speaker might choose to say the opening words as a single group: "If I speak with the tongues of men..." Another might prefer to make "and if I have all *faith*" into two groups: "and *if*... I have all *faith*." Whatever choices are made, all speakers at all times should avoid what we may call the "Beethoven Fifth Effect": Duh, Duh, Duh, Dumb: returning to the same low note at the end of every phrase or sentence—perhaps the most common single fault committed by those who read aloud. Readers should seek to vary their lower pitches, generally reserving the lowest pitch for the conclusion of a sequence of thoughts. Here is what Cicely Berry, voice and speech coach for the Royal Shakespeare Company, has to say about intonation: " Modern speech patterns are very often downward, and so in a sense introvert: but there is a different music in heightened speech which is to do with on-going energy, and so we need to be conscious of an upward movement. This applies to modern text as well. And this is not just a matter of using upward inflections—that is merely technical and will become automatic and ultimately boring—it is feeling, a physical impulse which impels you from one line to the next, one thought to the next, and this makes for a different cadence."[16]

Lesson Two: Stress Groups. In addition to intonation groups, English has patterns of stress that also fall into groups. There are usually several stress groups in an intonation group. Here are some very *useful guidelines to the patterns of stress in English*:

- All multi-syllabled words have one stressed syllable; the rest are unstressed. The dictionary is the authority: pro**phe**tic, **my**steries, a**bide**, re**joi**ces.
- All one-syllable nouns, verbs, adjectives and adverbs are always stressed: **love, gong, tongues, child**. So are **no** and **not**.
- Pronouns and prepositions, auxiliary verbs, conjunctions, and articles are usually unstressed. In certain contexts, however, they need to be stressed: "it's not on the table, it's **under** the table." "I didn't do it. **She** did."
- A stress group contains one stressed syllable, at least one, and only one—and the unstressed syllables that belong to it.
- Stress is indicated by length, pitch, and intensity.
- There is one change of pitch on every stressed syllable.
- In speaking a line, make a firm distinction between stressed and unstressed syllables. Get off the shorts and on to the longs. However, do not rush the unstressed words (a common tendency).

Here is the first movement again. The stressed syllables are in bold. The stress groups are indicated by a slash, the intonation groups by a double slash:

*If I **speak** //*
  *in the **tongues** / of **men** //*
  *and of **angels**, //*
*but have **not** / **love**, //*
*I am a **noi**sy / **gong** //*
  *or a **clang**ing / **cym**bal. //*
*And if I **have** / **prophe**tic / **powers**, //*
*and under**stand** / **all** / **mysteries** //*

and **all** / *knowledge,* //
and if I **have** / **all** / *faith,* //
*so as to re*__move__ / *moun*__tains,__ /
but have **not** / *love,* //
I am **no**thing. //
If I **give** / *away* //
all / *I* **have** /
*and If I de*liver //
my **bo**dy / *to be* **burned** //
but **have** / **not** / *love* //
I **gain** / **no**thing. //

EXERCISES FOR STRESS

- Speak the text while seated, accenting the stressed syllables.
- Still seated, with alternating feet, tap lightly on the unstressed syllables, heavily on the stressed syllables as you speak.
- Repeat the exercise, being careful to speak each stressed syllable in a phrase on a different pitch. Don't be afraid to exaggerate the pitch changes. *Usually, the most important word in the phrase will get the highest pitch: the last word of an intonation group. The exception is the last word of a sentence, often the most important word in the sentence. It is generally spoken on a lower pitch.*
- Stand up and walk, speaking the text. Step lightly on the unstressed syllables, heavily on the stressed. Plant

your foot as you speak the stressed syllable, drawing out the syllable slightly. Shift directions at each
punctuation mark.

- Repeat the exercise, moving more quickly and freely,
almost as if you were dancing. Feel the momentum of
each phrase as it moves toward the final word in the
phrase. Make a little gesture, such as a flourish of the
hand, on the last word, and then quickly shift direction for the next phrase.
- Stand and speak the passage as if to another person as
conversationally as you can, preserving the work on
stress and pitch.

Lesson Three. Taking the analysis of section one as a guide,
analyze the remaining sections into intonation and stress
groups. Repeat the exercises.

Lesson Four: Clarity. Our Elizabethan schoolmasters advise
us to speak our words "audibly, leisurely, distinctly, and naturally, sounding out especially the last syllable, that each word
may be understood." If readers of scripture would do only
this one thing, they would take a giant step toward engaging
our attention.

- Audibly: in our minds, we need to be speaking to the
back of the room. Even if we are using a microphone,
we need to reach out vocally toward the last row of
the congregation. Too many readers are not conscious of the space that surrounds them. When you
read, always take in the space you are in before looking down at the text and starting to speak. Engage the
whole congregation.

- Leisurely: we need to take one word at a time. Even the lowliest preposition and indefinite article are necessary for the clarity of the whole. A very good exercise for achieving this is to practice building up a phrase one word at a time: "if / if I / if I speak / if I speak in / if I speak in the / if I speak in the tongues…" Do not rush.
- Distinctly: there is nothing that frustrates the listener more than slurred and swallowed words. Work the muscles of the tongue and lips. Practice silently mouthing the text, prolonging the vowels and exaggerating the consonants. Then speak the text retaining the clarity of articulation. Do this again and again. Do it as your last minute practice before the service begins.
- Naturally: we want to sound like someone talking spontaneously, finding his or her words in the moment, and not like someone reading a lesson.
- Clearly: sounding out the word, especially the last syllable. Perhaps the most common fault of readers in the liturgy is to drop the last syllable or consonant of a word. We need to keep the vocal energy moving through the whole word. Similarly, we need to avoid dropping the ends of phrases and sentences. The important information of a phrase or a sentence almost always comes at the end.[8]
- In our literate culture we tend to think of words as something on a page, something we look up in a dictionary. But of course words are first of all sequences of sound. These sounds are not arbitrary. They need to be fully spoken if the words are to have their full impact.

Lesson Five: Parenthetical Material. To speak a text clearly, to make the thought "manifest," is largely a matter of "observing one's distinctions," of not flattening everything into monotone. In the above exercises, we have been practicing making distinctions between intonation groups, and between stress groups. In addition, we need to make distinctions between the principal thrust of a sentence and the parenthetical material. For example, in the following phrase, "so as to move mountains" is parenthetical: "if I have all faith

Table 12.2

The Melody of Thought. Engaged speech has melody. The melodic patterns of thought are in fact quite similar to those of song. Songs are written in **keys**. The note that determines the key is called the **tonic**. The tonic note of the key of C is C. Traditional songs tend to end on the tonic note. The return to the tonic at the end of a song indicates closure. The phrases of a song are similar to the intonation groups of speech: a note higher than the tonic (or occasionally lower) at the end of a musical phrase signals that the lyric thought is continuing. For instance, if a song is written in the key of C, the first phrase might end in D, the second in E, the third in G, and the fourth in C (end of a sequence of thoughts). In addition, the high notes of a song tend to be reserved for particularly significant or emotionally charged words. The vowels of these words tend to be held longer. In the following exercises we will suggest something of the melodic flow of the words with letters, A indicating the lowest pitch, G the highest. These are only suggestions. Individual speakers might phrase the words quite differently. The thing to remember is: *the prosodic, or melodic characteristics of speech make the thought clear.* This concern with melodic flow applies both to single clauses within a sentence, whole sentences, and several sentences in sequences. That is, while we may (but not always) lower the pitch at the ends of sentences, we want to reserve the lowest pitch (the "tonic") to signal the end of a sequence of thoughts.

(so as to remove mountains) but have not love, I am nothing." We could leave the parenthesis out and the sentence
would still make sense. The usual way of indicating parenthetical material with the voice is to lower the pitch and pick
up the pace just slightly, then resume the higher pitch and
the slower pace when we return to the main thrust of the
sentence.

- If "a" is the lowest note, and "g" is the highest note,
  speak the following phrase making the distinction
  between the parenthetical material and the main sentence clear through the use of pitch:

  >   c   d   e
  > if I have all *faith*,
  >   a   a   b
  > (so as to remove *mountains*)
  >   c   f g
  > but have not *love*, /
  >   c   d
  > I am *nothing*. /

Speak the sentence several times until making the parenthetical distinction clear feels easy and natural.

- Practice making the parenthetical distinctions clear
  with the following phrases from the Second Chapter
  of Galatians:

  1. Yet we know / that a person is justified / (not by
     the works of the law) but through faith in Jesus
     Christ.

2. But if, / (in our effort / to be justified in Christ,) we ourselves have been found / to be sinners, / is Christ then / a servant of sin?

Lesson Six: Oppositions. When we speak, we frequently oppose one thing to another: good vs. evil, sweet vs. sorrow, and so on. Our usual way of making the distinction clear is again through contrasting pitches.

- Speak the following phrases, making a clear distinction between the things opposed:

        a   e   f   d   c   b
    Love is patient and kind; love is not jealous or boastful...

        a   c   b   e   b
    For our knowledge is imperfect and our prophecy is imperfect

        a   b   f   d   b   a   c
    But when the perfect comes, the imperfect will pass away...

        a   c   b   b+   c-   g   d   e
    For now we see in a mirror dimly, but then face to face...

- Corinthians 13 is full of subtle distinctions, even when things are not directly opposed. Look, for example, at the opening phrase. There is clearly a distinction to be made between "the tongues of men and of angels" and "a noisy gong or a clanging cymbal." The speaker needs to find the "melody of thought," the variations in pitch and stress that will make the meaning manifest.

Lesson Seven: Rhetoric, Syntax and Momentum (Section 1). Syntax need not only map out the logical structure of a thought. It can also be expressive. Section 1 is a masterly example of how a writer—especially one trained in Classical Rhetoric—can manipulate syntax to intensify the force and momentum of what he or she is saying.[9] Paul achieves this primarily through the use of three rhetorical figures:

a) *Anaphora,* repeating the same word or words at the beginning of successive clauses or sentences: "if I speak…if I have…if I give, etc."

b) *Polysyndeton,* the generous use of conjunctions: "and if I have…and understand all mysteries and all knowledge, etc."

c) *Auxesis,* a build. Raising the stakes with a succession of words or clauses of increasing importance: "tongues of men and of angels…all prophecy…all mysteries…all knowledge, all faith," and finally the climactic giving away of "all I have" and the burning of my body. Note also the repetition of "all," which reinforces the sense of *auxesis.*

To the attentive speaker, the syntax of section 1 indicates the need for a *crescendo* in which successive clauses build on the preceding ones.

> If I speak in the tongues of men and of angels, but have not love, I am a noisy gong or a clanging cymbal.
>
> And if I have prophetic powers, and understand all mysteries and all knowledge, and if I have all faith, so as to remove mountains, but have not love, I am nothing.
>
> If I give away all I have and if I deliver my body to be burned, but have not love, I gain nothing.

The speaker needs to feel and suggest the rising energy of the passage, giving each element of the build its distinctive intonation and degree of stress. Read the sentences a number of times, gradually "layering in" the rhetorical elements.

EXERCISES FOR SECTION ONE:

- Read the passage out loud, building the succeeding "if"-clauses: "if I speak" > "and if I have prophetic powers" > "and if I have all faith, etc."
- The generous use of "and" contributes to the deliberate momentum of the passage and emphasizes the impressive weight of all that is nothing without love. Read the passage again, dwelling slightly on the "ands."
- Build each of the clauses introduced by "and" through variations in pitch and emphasis. Don't reduce all the things balanced against love—"the tongues of men...prophetic powers...all mysteries and all knowledge, etc."—to a dull list. Give each its distinctive inflection. Think the meaning of each thing as you say the word.
- Make the pitch distinctions for the parenthetical material ("so as to remove mountains"), and the oppositions (men/angels, tongues/noisy gong, etc.) The most important opposition, of course, is that between "love" and all that is balanced against it.
- Notice that this section has a short refrain, composed of four stressed monosyllables: "but have not love."

It is repeated three times. This simple refrain has an insistent, almost doom-like stress that contrasts with the more expansive preceding clauses. Give each successive repetition of "love" a subtle lift in pitch. This will give a sense of the swelling power of love.

- Notice that the final, main clauses of the sentences are also an example of *anaphora* ("I am…I am…I gain. .."). The refrain-like repetition of the same syntactical structure at the end of each sentence gives the section a mounting sense of finality. This is reinforced by a subtle progression from the metaphoric "noisy gong and clanging cymbal…" to "nothing" to "gain nothing." The monosyllabic main verb, "gain," in the concluding sentence contrasts strongly with the unstressed "am" of the preceding main clauses. The strong stress on "gain" tends to increase the stress on the first syllable of the final "**no**thing."

I am a noisy gong or a clanging cymbal.
I am nothing.
I gain nothing.

Lesson Eight: Repetition and Variation (Section 2). We have already noticed Paul's artful use of repetition and variation. The art of the speaker needs to match the art of the writer. The speaker must "observe his [or her] distinctions," convey through inflection the slight shift of meaning and emphasis of each repetition. Notice, for instance, the play of repetition and variation in section 2, composed in twelve short, syntactically similar clauses, each detailing an aspect of the nature of love.

Love is patient and kind;
love is not jealous or boastful;
it is not arrogant or rude.
Love does not insist on its own way;
it is not irritable or resentful;
it does not rejoice at wrong,
but rejoices in the right.
Love bears all things,
believes all things,
hopes all things,
endures all things.
Love never ends…

Here are some things we need to consider in making our "distinctions" in section 2:

- The first word, "love," establishes a pattern of insistent repetition (the figure, *anaphora*). The word is repeated four times at the beginning of a clause, its substitute, "it," at the beginning of three.
- If we speak "love" and "it" on the same lower ("tonic") pitch, we will bring out this insistence on love.
- If we then enumerate the various qualities love does or does not have on higher, varied pitches, we will make the meaning "manifest:"

a   e   f   a   d c   b
Love is patient and kind / love is not jealous or boastful;

a   b d   c
it is not arrogant or rude.

- Notice that the "not" in the second clause is spoken on a higher pitch. The monosyllable "not"—according to our guidelines for prose stress—receives particular emphasis. But the fact that "not" also breaks the syntactic and rhythmic parallelism between the first two clauses reinforces the opposition between what love is and what love is not.

SENTENCE 2

- The second sentence is also composed of three independent clauses, but varies the established pattern by adding a subordinate clause at the end.
- The first clause—beginning with "love"—resumes the *anaphora* of the opening sentence. However, for the first time Paul uses an active verb ("does not insist") rather than the verb "to be." The clause also, for the first time, varies the length of the phrase.
- The second clause, on the other hand, parallels the third clause of the first sentence. It introduces a variation on the *anaphora* ("it" for "love").
- The third clause echoes the first clause by also using an active verb, "rejoice."
- The fourth (subordinate) clause of the sentence—strongly marked by its coordinating conjunction "but"—is a striking and concluding turn on the opening sequence of six independent clauses. It is the first clause since the opening that is not in the negative. It concludes with a triumphal affirmation that also opposes right to wrong. The repetition of "rejoice"

in the concluding clause—this time in the affirmative—adds a note of celebration; as a repeated word it demands particular emphasis.

SENTENCE 3

- The third sentence of the passage takes a new tack. It renews the continuing use of *anaphora* (the repetition of "love" at the beginning of a succession of clauses). It also introduces a syntactic variation: a sequence of four active verbs, each depending on a single subject.[10]
- Notice that each of the four verbs "raises the stakes" (*auxesis*): "bears>believes>hopes>endures." If we give each verb its distinctive pitch, we will make this progression clear and suggest something of the power of love.
- In contrast to the mounting force of the four verbs is the repetition of their direct object, "all things."[11] We might speak each of these repetitions on the same pitch, with a special insistence on the final "all things." The thought might be "scored" something like this:

   a   b   a   a   c   a   a   d   a   a
Love bears all things, believes all things, hopes all things,

   a   e   a   a
endures *all things*.

- The repetition of "all things," in conjunction with the mounting succession of verbs, gives the sentence a distinctive vigor that prepares the final affirmation in the fourth sentence: "love never ends."

- Syntactically, of course, this last sentence is linked to the third and final movement. But it is also clear that this independent clause is the climactic affirmation of the whole chapter: love is transcendent; love is not subject to time.

Lesson Nine: Making One's Point. Each of the three sections of the chapter has its distinctive momentum; each is a stage in the momentum of the passage as a whole. This is another way of saying that each of the sections is moving toward its conclusion, or making its "point"—literally, since we end a sentence with a period.[12] Truly engaged thought, like melody, has momentum. On the one hand, thought finds its way, moves "moment to moment" in relatively short steps. On the other hand, thought is in search of its conclusion, and it is the intensity of this search that gives a sentence, a paragraph, a passage as a whole its energy. In the following exercises for the adventurous, we will literally seek to experience the movement of a thought toward "its point."

EXERCISES FOR THE MOVEMENT OF THOUGHT:

- Pick a point in the room. Speak the first sentence of Corinthians 1.13 as you move vigorously but deliberately toward that point. Do not allow the energy to flag as you speak the end of the sentence, but "make your point" as you reach your point: without love I am "A CLANGING CYMBAL."

- Speak the next sentence as you move on to your next point. Continue your progress sentence by sentence through the speech, moving in a different direction for each one. Be careful not to become a clanging cymbal: find the melody (vary the pitch) of the important stressed words. Do not hit the same low pitch at the end of every sentence.

Thought does not always move in a direct line toward its point. In finds its way, often twisting and turning even as it looks toward its conclusion.

- Pick a point in the room and head toward it as you begin to speak the sentence. However, each time you come to a punctuation mark, veer slightly off direction, still keeping the final point in sight. Zigzag your way to your conclusion.
- Each of the three sections builds toward its culminating point: 1) "I gain nothing." 2) "Love never ends." 3) "The greatest of these is love." Notice that the three points are in fact an *auxesis*, a progression.
- Move through each of the three sections in turn, sentence by sentence, toward its "main point." Feel how each thought, each sentence gathers momentum as you work your way toward a conclusion. Do the same with the whole passage, gathering momentum as you move toward the strongest affirmation of all: "The greatest of these is love."

Lesson Ten: Feigning to Speak. In conclusion, we should note that the art of *pronunciatio* is inherently dramatic, the reader a close cousin of the actor. The reader, like the actor, should seem actually to be talking, finding the words of the text in the moment, as if they were his or her own. The reader is, in a sense, impersonating the "voice of the text," the voice of the storyteller, the voice of the prophet, the voice of the apostle. The word "gospel" means "good news," coming from Old English, "*god* (good) *spell* (news, discourse, or story)." It is a translation of Late Latin "evangelium," also meaning "good news." In the word Evangel, we find the Greek words "eu-" ("good") and "angelos" ("messenger," or "mounted courier"). Thus, etymology suggests:

1) The speaker of the Gospel (or of scripture) is a bringer of news.
2) The news is urgent. The messenger is, as it were, on horseback.
3) The news is—perhaps uncharacteristically—good.
4) The news is delivered out loud.[13]

Scripture, then, is the written record of what was originally spoken by the messenger. To read scripture out loud is, in a sense, to assume the role of the messenger, to deliver news that is both urgent and good: "Christ has died, Christ has risen, Christ will come again."[14] What does it mean "to assume the role of the messenger?" Walter Ong has spoken of the "evocative quality," the "calling quality," of great literature. "Literature," according to Ong, "exists in a context of one presence calling to another," and—as Christopher Bryan has shown us—Scripture, in addition to being sacred text, is also great literature.[15] Like literature, scripture is oral in essence. It comes truly to life as utterance.

As readers in the liturgy, we are appointed to listen with humility and deep attention to the call or cry of the text and to give it voice. We are called to become messengers, to rediscover—to recognize—what was originally urgent and provocative in the scripted words, and to speak them, delivering, as if for the first time, what has not yet been fully heard: "the news."

Notes

1. Walter J. Ong, S. J., *The Barbarian Within* (NY: Macmillan, 2nd Printing, 1968), p. 58.
2. See George A. Kennedy, *Classical Rhetoric & Its Christian and Secular Tradition* (Chapel Hill: The University of North Carolina Press, 2nd edition, 1999). Technically, *Pronunciatio* is the fifth part of Classical Rhetoric: the art of delivering a speech. Skill in speaking text was considered essential to the training of an orator. *Pronunciatio* was also called *Actio*, or action. As the word suggests, this fifth part of rhetoric has traditionally been associated with the art of the actor. Both Cicero and Quintilian advised the young orator to study actors, even to employ an actor as teacher.
3. This collage of citations is taken from Bertram Joseph's *Acting Shakespeare* (NY: Theatre Arts Books, 2nd Edition, 1969), Chapter 1, "The Schoolboy and the Actor," pp. 1–19. They are from such renowned Elizabethan and Jacobean writers and schoolmasters as William Kempe, John Brinsley, and Richard Mulcaster.
4. The technical word for the musicality of speech is **prosody**. Speech has rhythm, melody, tone, pitch, and stress. Prosody comes from *aoide,* the Greek word for song.
5. Scripture quotations are from Revised Standard Version of the Bible, copyright © 1946, 1952, and 1971 National Council of the Churches of Christ in the United States of America. Used by permission. All rights reserved.
6. "Anyone who listens objectively to speech will quickly notice that it is not produced in continuous, uninterrupted flow but in spurts...If we think of a typical substantive intonation

unit as having the form of a clause, and if we think of a clause as verbalizing the idea of an event or state, we can conclude that each such idea is active, occupies a focus of consciousness, for only a brief time, each being replaced by another idea at roughly one-to two second intervals." Wallace Chafe, *Discourse, Consciousness, and Time: The Flow and Displacement of Conscious Experience in Speaking and Writing* (The University of Chicago Press, 1994), p. 61.

7. Some of the exercises I have invented, some I have adapted from exercises learned from my teachers. I owe a particular debt to Patsy Rodenburg, who has been my mentor in these matters for some time. Her books are particularly helpful for anyone wishing to learn the art of *pronunciatio.* See especially *The Need for Words* (London: Methuen, 1994), and *Speaking Shakespeare* (New York: Palgrave MacMillan, 2004).

8. "A substantive intonation unit usually (though not always) conveys some new information. What we have seen so far is that the new information is not likely to reside in the subject of a clause. To the extent that an intonation unit adheres to the clause format, then, the locus of new information is in the predicate." Chafe, p. 108.

9. Obviously, in analyzing the syntax and rhetoric of the passage, we are basing our analysis on a translation, not on Paul's Greek. For our purposes, however, we will assume that the translation is more or less faithful to the original.

10. This is the figure, *diazeugma*: a succession of verbs depending on a single subject.

11. The figure, *epistrophe*: the opposite of *anaphora*, the same word or words repeated at the end of a succession of clauses.

12. In French, a period is in fact called "un point." A witty conclusion is called "une pointe," as in the point of a knife.

13. "Faith," as Paul points out, "comes from what is heard" (Rom. 10.17). Clement of Rome, writing toward the end of the first Christian century, does not say that the Apostles went into the world to write letters or gospels, but rather, "they went forth in the assurance of the Holy Spirit preaching the good news (*euangelizomenoi*) that the Kingdom of God is coming. They proclaimed (*kērussantes*) from district to district, and from city to city" (1 Clem. 42.3-4a).

14. Interestingly, this central affirmation of the Christian faith is an example of *auxesis*.
15. Ong, p. 58.
16. Cicely Berry, *The Actor and His Text* (New York: Scribner's, 1988), p. 33.

SELECT BIBLIOGRAPHY

Aitken, Ellen Bradshaw. See Playoust, Catherine.

Alexander, Philip S. "Hellenism and Hellenization as Problematic Historiographical Categories." In *Paul Beyond the Judaism/Hellenism Divide*, Troels Engberg-Pedersen, ed. Louisville: Westminster John Knox, 2001. 63–80.

Allison, C. FitzSimons. "The Incarnate Word and the Written Word." In *Sewanee Theological Review* **55**.3 (2012): 279–92.

Alter, Robert. *The Art of Biblical Narrative*. New York: Basic Books, 1981.

Auerbach, Erich. *Mimesis: Dargestellte Wirklichkeit in der abendländischen Literatur.*Basle: A. Francke, 1946. ET: *Mimesis: The Representation of Reality in Western Literature*, Willard R. Trask, trans. Princeton: Princeton University, 1953.

Baldwin, T. W. *William Shakespere's Small Latine and Lesse Greek*. Champaign, Ill.: University of Illinois, 1944.

Barth, Karl. *Die kirchliche Dogmatik.*Zollikon, Zürich: Verlag der Evangelischen Buchhandlung, 1939-70. ET: *Church Dogmatics*, G. W. Bromiley, T. F. Torrance, ed. and transl. Edinburgh: T. & T. Clark, 1956-77.

Bate, Jonathan. *Soul of the Age: A Biography of the Mind of William Shakespeare*. New York: Random House, 2009.

Bauckham, Richard. *Women in the Gospels: Studies of the Named Women in the Gospels*. Grand Rapids, Mich.: Eerdmans, 2002.

Benedict XVI. See Ratzinger, Joseph.

Benz, Arnold. *Die Zukunft des Universums: Zufall, Chaos, Gott?* Düsseldorf: Patmos Verlag, 1997. ET: *The Future of the Universe: Chance, Chaos, God?* New York: Continuum, 2000.

Bianchi, Enzo. *Pregare la parola. Introduzione alla "Lectio divina."* Milan: Gribaudi, 1970. ET: *Praying the Word: An Introduction to Lectio Divina*, James W. Zona, transl. Kalamazoo, Michigan: Cistercian Publications, 1998.

Bockmuehl, Markus. *Seeing the Word: Refocusing New Testament Study*. Grand Rapids, Mich.: Baker Academic, 2006.

Borg, Marcus. *Jesus: Uncovering the Life, Teachings, and Relevance of a Religious Revolutionary*. New York: HarperCollins, 2006.

Brettler, Marc Zvi. See Harrington, Daniel J., S. J.

Brown, David. *Tradition and Imagination: Revelation and Change*. Oxford: Oxford University Press, 1999.

———. *Discipleship and Imagination: Christian Tradition and Truth*. Oxford: Oxford University Press, 2000.

Browning, Robert. "A Death in the Desert." 1864. In Robert Browning, *Dramatis personae*. Boston: Ticknor and Fields, 1864. 101–132.

Brueggemann, Walter. *Genesis*. Atlanta: John Knox Press, 1982.

———. *Theology of the Old Testament: Testimony, Dispute, Advocacy*. Minneapolis: Fortress, 1997.

Bryan, Christopher. *A Preface to Romans: Notes on the Epistle in Its Literary and Social Setting*. Oxford: Oxford University Press, 2000.

———. *And God Spoke: The Authority of the Bible for the Church Today*. Cambridge, Mass.: Cowley, 2002.

———. *Render to Caesar: Jesus, the Early Church, and the Roman Superpower*. Oxford: Oxford University Press, 2005.

———. *The Resurrection of the Messiah*. Oxford: Oxford University Press, 2011.

———. "C. S. Lewis as a Reader of Scripture." In *A Sewanee Companion to "The Cambridge Companion to C. S. Lewis,"* Robert MacSwain, ed., *Sewanee Theological Review* **55**.2 (2012): 180–207; also available online at http://christopherbry-anonline.com/articles/cs-lewis-and-the-bible/.

Burke, Seàn. *The Death and Return of the Author.* Edinburgh: Edinburgh University, 1992.

The Cambridge Companion to C. S. Lewis, Robert MacSwain and Michael Ward, eds. Cambridge: Cambridge University: 2010.

Charles Darwin and the Tree of Life and *Darwin's Struggle—The Evolution of the Origin of Species.* DVD: BBC Earth, 2009.

Childs, Brevard S. *The Book of Exodus.* Louisville, Ky.: Westminster John Knox, 1974.

Coleridge, Samuel Taylor. *Biographia Literaria.* 2 vols. 1817. Text in James Engell and W. Jackson Bate, *The Collected Works of Samuel Taylor Coleridge: Biographia Literaria.* Princeton: Princeton University, 1983.

Crossan, John Dominic. *The Cross that Spoke: The Origins of the Passion Narrative.* San Francisco: Harper and Row, 1988.

———. *The Historical Jesus: The Life of a Mediterranean Jewish Peasant.* San Francisco: HarperCollins / Edinburgh: T. & T. Clark, 1991.

———. *A Long Way from Tipperary: A Memoir.* New York: Harper SanFrancisco, 2000.

Crysdale, Cynthia and Neil Ormerod, *Creator God, Evolving World.* Minneapolis: Fortress Press, 2013.

Cunningham, Valentine. "Best Stories in the Best Order? Canons, Apocryphas, and (Post) Modern Reading." In *Literature and Theology 14*.1 (2000). 69–80.

Dante Alighieri. *Commedia.* c1308-1321. Text in Anna Maria Chiavacci Leonardi, *Dante Alighieri Commedia.* 3 vols. Milan: Arnoldo Mondadori, 1991–97. Text and translation in Alan Mandelbaum, *The Divine Comedy of Dante Alighieri.* 3 vols. Norwalk, Conn.: The Easton Press, 2001.

Darwin, Charles. *On the Origin of Species by Means of Natural Selection, or the Preservation of Favoured Races in the Struggle for Life.* London: John Murray, 1859. For the 6th edition (1872), the title was changed to *The Origin of Species.*

Davey, Noel. See Hoskyns, Sir Edwyn.

Dawkins, Richard. *The God Delusion.* Boston: Houghton Mifflin, 2006.

Dilthey, Wilhelm, *Selected Writings*, ed. H. P. Rickman. Cambridge: Cambridge University, 1976.

Downing, F. Gerald. *Cynics and Christian Origins.* Edinburgh: T. & T. Clark, 1992.

Dryden, John. *Absalom and Achitophel*.1681. Text in W. D. Christie revised by C. H. Firth, *Dryden: Absalom & Achitophel*, 5th edition. Oxford: Clarendon, 1911.

Dunn, J. D. G. *Jesus Remembered*. Grand Rapids, Mich. / Cambridge, England: Eerdmans, 2003.

Eco, Umberto, and Cardinal Carlo Maria Martini. *In cosa crede che non crede*.Florence: Liberal libri, 1996. ET: *Belief or Nonbelief: A Confrontation*, Minna Proctor, transl. New York: Arcade, 1997.

Ehrman, Bart D. *The Lost Christianities: The Battles for Scripture and the Faiths We Never Knew*. New York: Oxford University Press, 2003.

Enns, Peter. See Harrington, Daniel J., S. J. *Essays Catholic and Critical*, Edward Gordon Selwyn, ed. London: Society for Promoting Christian Knowledge, 1926.

Fiorenza, Elisabeth Schüssler. *In Memory of Her: A Feminist Reconstruction of Christian Origins*. New York: Crossroad, 1984.

The Five Gospels. R. W. Funk, R. W. Hoover, and the Jesus Seminar, eds. New York: MacMillan, 1993.

Fowl, Stephen E. *Engaging Scripture: A Model for Theological Interpretation*. Oxford: Blackwell, 1998.

Frei, Hans W. "Theological Reflections on the Accounts of Jesus' Death and Resurrection." In *The Christian Scholar* **49**: 4 (1966) 263–306; reprinted in Frei, *Theology and Narrative: Selected Essays*, George Hunsinger and William C. Placher, eds. New York and Oxford: Oxford University Press, 1991. 45–94 esp. 86–87.

Frye, Northrop. *The Great Code: The Bible and Literature*. San Diego: Harcourt, 1981.

Funk, Robert W. "The Issue of Jesus." In *Forum* **1**.1 (March, 1985): 7–12.

Gatta, John. *The Transfiguration of Christ and Creation*. Eugene, Oregon: Wipf and Stock, 2011.

Greer, Rowan A. *Anglican Approaches to Scripture*. New York: Herder and Herder, 2006.

Hanson, Paul D. *The Diversity of Scripture*. Philadelphia: Fortress, 1982.

Harrington, Daniel J., S. J. "Reading the Bible Critically and Religiously," and Peter Enns's "Response." In Marc Zvi Brettler,

Peter Enns, and Daniel Harrington, S. J., *The Bible and the Believer: How to Read the Bible Critically and Religiously*. Oxford: Oxford University Press, 2012. 80–118.

Harris, Carol. *Women at War: The Home Front 1939–1945*. Stroud: Sutton Publishing, 2000.

———. *Women at War in Uniform 1939–1945*. Stroud: Sutton Publishing, 2002.

Haskell, David George. *The Forest Unseen: A Year's Watch in Nature*. New York: Viking, 2012.

Hays, Richard B. *The Moral Vision of the New Testament: A Contemporary Introduction to New Testament Ethics*. San Francisco: HarperSanFrancisco, 1996.

Heisenberg, Werner. *Physics and philosophy: The Revolution in Modern Science*. New York: Harper and Row, 1962.

Holderness, Graham. *Nine Lives of William Shakespeare*. London: Continuum, 2011.

Homan, Lynn M., and Thomas Reilly. *Black Knights: The Story of the Tuskegee Airmen*. Gretna, Louisiana: Pelican, 2001.

Hope, Jonathan. *Shakespeare Language: Reason, Eloquence and Artifice in the Renaissance*, Arden Shakespeare. London: Methuen Drama A. & C. Black, 2010.

Horsley, Richard. *Jesus and Empire: The Kingdom of God and the New World Disorder*. Minneapolis: Fortress, 2003.

Hoskyns, Sir Edwyn. "Christ of the Synoptic Gospels." In *Essays Catholic and Critical by Members of the Anglican Communion*. Edward Gordon Selwyn, ed. London: S.P.C.K., 1926. 151–78.

———. and Noel Davey. *The Riddle of the New Testament*. London: Faber and Faber, 1931; rev. 1936.

Hughes, Robert D., III. *Beloved Dust: Tides of the Spirit in the Christian Life*. New York: Continuum, 2008.

James, John. *Chartres: The Masons Who Built a Legend*. London: Routledge and Kegan Paul, 1982.

Jenson, Robert W. *Systematic Theology*.2 vols. Oxford and New York: Oxford University Press, 1997–99.

———. *Canon and Creed*. Louisville, Ky.: Westminster John Knox, 2010.

Jesus' Resurrection Fact or Figment?: A Debate Between William Lane Craig and Gerd Lüdemann, Paul Copan and Ronald K. Tacelli, eds. Downers Grove, Illinois: InterVarsity Press, 2000.

Johnson, Luke Timothy. *The Real Jesus: The Misguided Quest for the Historical Jesus and the Truth of the Traditional Gospels.* San Francisco: HarperSanFrancisco, 1996.

Jowett, Benjamin. "On the Interpretation of Scripture." In *Essays and Reviews*, 8th ed. London: Longman, Green, Longman and Roberts, 1861 [1860]. 334–78.

Kaufman, Gordon D. *In Face of Mystery: A Constructive Theology.* Cambridge, Mass.: Harvard University Press, 1993.

Keegan, John E. "Reflections on the Priesthood after Reading Julia Gatta's *The Nearness of God.*" In *Sewanee Theological Review* 55:4 (2012): 403–411.

Keener, Craig S. *The Historical Jesus of the Gospels.* Grand Rapids, Mich.: Eerdmans, 2009.

Kelly, J. N. D. *Early Christian Creeds.* London: Longmans, Green, and Co., 1950.

Kennedy, George. "Classical and Christian Source Criticism." In *The Relationships Among the Gospels: An Interdisciplinary Dialogue.* William O. Walker, Jr., ed. Trinity University Monograph Series in Religion 5. San Antonio, Texas: Trinity University Press, 1978. 125–55.

Koester, Helmut. "Gnomai Diaphorai." In James M. Robinson and Helmut Koester, *Trajectories Through Early Christianity.* Philadelphia: Fortress, 1971. 114–57.

Kristeva, Julia. *Semeiōtichē: Recherches pour une sémanalyse.* Paris: Seuil, 1969; and *Polylogue.* Paris: Seuil, 1977. ET: *Desire in Language: A Semiotic Approach to Literature and Art*, Leon S. Roudiez, ed., Thomas Gora, Alice Jardine, and Leon S. Roudiez, transl. New York: Columbia University Press, 1980.

———. *La Révolution du langage poétique.* Paris: Seuil, 1974.

LaCocque, André. *Le Livre de Ruth.* Commentaire de l'Ancien Testament 13. Geneva: Labor et Fides, 2004. ET (revised and expanded by the author) *Ruth*, K. C. Hanson, trans. Minneapolis: Fortress, 2004.

———. *The Captivity of Innocence: Babel and the Yahwist.* Eugene: Cascade, 2010.

Legaspi, Michael. *The Death of Scripture and the Rise of Biblical Studies.* Oxford: Oxford University Press, 2010.

Levenson, Jon D. *Sinai and Zion: An Entry to the Jewish Bible.* New York: Winston Press, 1985.

Levering, Matthew. *Participatory Biblical Exegesis: A Theology of Biblical Interpretation.* Notre Dame, Ind.: University of Notre Dame Press, 2008.

Lewis, C. S. *The Abolition of Man: Reflections on education with special reference to the teaching of English in the upper forms of schools.* Oxford: Oxford University, revised edition 1946 (1943).

———. *Miracles: A Preliminary Study.* London: Geoffrey Bles, 1947; revised 1960.

———. *The Voyage of the Dawn Treader.* London: Geoffrey Bles, 1952.

———. *The Last Battle.* London: Bodley Head, 1956.

———. *An Experiment in Criticism.* Cambridge: Cambridge University Press, 1961.

———. "Modern Theology and Biblical Criticism." In *Christian Reflections*, Walter Hooper, ed. Grand Rapids, Mich.: Eerdmans, 1967, 152–66. Republished as "Fern-seed and Elephants" in *Fern-seed and Elephants and Other Essays on Christianity* by C. S. Lewis, Walter Hooper, ed. Glasgow: William Collins, Fontana, 1975. 104–25.

———. "Meditation in a Toolshed." In *God in the Dock: Essays on Theology and Ethics*, Walter Hooper, ed. Grand Rapids, Mich.: Eerdmans, 1970. 212–15.

Louth, Andrew. *Discerning the Mystery: An Essay on the Nature of Theology.* Oxford: Clarendon, 1983.

de Lubac, Henri. *Exégèse Médiévale, 1: Les quatres sens de l'écriture* (Paris: Montaigne, 1959); ET *Medieval Exegesis, 1, The Four Senses of Scripture*, Mark Sebank, transl. (Grand Rapids, Mich.: William B. Eerdmans / Edinburgh: T. & T. Clark, 1998).

Lux Mundi: A Series of Studies on the Religion of the Incarnation, Charles Gore, ed. 10th edition. London: John Murray, 1891 [1889].

MacCulloch, Diarmaid. *A History of Christianity: The First Three Thousand Years.*London: Allen Lane, 2010 / *Christianity: The First Three Thousand Years.* New York: Viking, 2010.

Macdonald, George. *Phantastes.*London: Smith, Elder and Co.,1858.

———. *Lilith.*London: Chatto and Windus, 1895.

Mack, Burton. *A Myth of Innocence: Mark and Christian Origins*. Philadelphia: Fortress, 1988.

Martin, Dale B. "Paul and the Judaism/Hellenism Dichotomy." In *Paul Beyond the Judaism/Hellenism Divide*, Troels Engberg-Pedersen, ed. Louisville: Westminster John Knox, 2001. 33–44.

———. *Pedagogy of the Bible: An Analysis and Proposal*. Louisville, Ky.: Westminster John Knox, 2008.

Meier, John P. *A Marginal Jew; Rethinking the Historical Jesus*. 4 vols. Anchor/Yale, 1991–2009.

Merz, Annette: see Theissen, Gerd.

Metzger, Bruce M. *A Textual Commentary on the Greek New Testament: A Companion Volume to the United Bible Societies Greek New Testament, 3rd edition*. London and New York: United Bible Societies, 1975.

Moberly, R. W. L. *The Bible, Theology, and Faith: A Study of Abraham and Jesus*. Cambridge: Cambridge University Press, 2000.

Moore, Aubrey "The Christian Doctrine of God." In *Lux Mundi: A Series of Studies on the Religion of the Incarnation*, Charles Gore, ed. 10th edition. London: John Murray, 1891 [1889]. 41–81.

Napier, B. David. *From Faith to Faith: Essays on Old Testament Literature*. New York: Harper, 1955.

Nelson, Marilyn. "Translator's Preface." In *Euripides, 1, Hecuba*, David R. Slavitt and Palmer Bovie, eds. Philadelphia: University of Philadelphia Press, 1998. 73–75.

Ong, S. J., Walter. *The Presence of the Word: Some Prolegomena for Cultural and Religious History*. Yale: Yale University Press, 1967.

———. *Interfaces of the Word: Studies in the Evolution of Consciousness and Culture*. Ithaca and London: Cornell University, 1977.

Ormerod, Neil. "'Questions in Understanding Divine Action." In *Sewanee Theological Review* 56.4 (2013): 337–46.

———. See Crysdale, Cynthia.

Pagola, José A. *Jesús. Aproximación histórica*.Madrid: PPC, 2007. ET: *Jesus: A Historical Approximation*. Miami, Fla.: Convivium, 2009.

Parry, Milman. "The Historical Method in Literary Criticism." In *The Making of Homeric Verse: The Collected Papers of*

Milman Parry, ed. Adam Parry. New York and Oxford: Oxford University Press, 1987. 408–13. Reprinted from *HAB* **38** (1936): 778–82.

Pearson, Birger A. "The Gospel According to the Jesus Seminar." In *Religion* **25** (1995): 317–38.

Pervo, Richard I. *Dating Acts: Between the Evangelists and the Apologists*. Santa Rosa: Polebridge, 2006.

Phillips, Denise. *Acolytes of Nature: Defining Natural Science in Germany, 1770–1850*.Chicago: University of Chicago Press, 2012.

Playoust, Catherine, and Ellen Bradshaw Aitken, "The Leaping Child: Imagining the Unborn in Early Christian Literature." In Vanessa R. Sasson and Jane Marie Law, eds. *Imagining the Fetus: The Unborn in Myth, Religion, and Culture*. AAR Cultural Criticism Series. Oxford; Oxford University Press, 2009. 157–84.

Proust, Marcel. *À la recherche du temps perdu, 1, Du coté de chez Swann*. Paris: Gallimard, 1913.

Ratzinger, Joseph (afterwards Benedict XVI). *Schriftauslegung im Widerstreit*, QD 117. Freiburg im Breisgau: Herder, 1989.

Reilly, Thomas. See Homan, Lynn M.

Ricoeur, Paul. "Herméneutique de l'idée de Révélation" (1977). In *Ecrits et conférences. 2. Herméneutique de Paul Ricoeur, Daniel Frey et Nicola Stricker*.Paris: Seuil, 2010. ET: "Toward a Hermeneutic of the Idea of Revelation," David Pellauer, transl. In *Paul Ricoeur: Essays on Biblical Interpretation*, Lewis S. Mudge, ed. Philadelphia: Fortress, 1990. 77–81.

———. "Interpretative Narrative," David Pellauer, transl. In *The Book and the Text: The Bible and Literary Theory*, Regina Schwartz, ed. Oxford: Basil Blackwell, 1990. 236–57.

Robinson, James M. See Koester, Helmut.

Robinson, Marilynne. *Home*. New York: Farrar, Straus, and Giroux, 2008.

———. *Absence of Mind: The Dispelling of Inwardness from the Modern Myth of the Self*. New Haven: Yale University, 2010.

———. *When I Was a Child I Read Books*. New York: Farrar, Strauss and Giroux, 2012.

Rodenburg, Patsy. *Speaking Shakespeare*. London and New York: Palgrave Macmillan, 2002.

Sanders, James A. *From Sacred Story to Sacred Text: Canon as Paradigm*. Philadelphia: Fortress, 1987.

Sanders, E. P. *Jesus and Judaism*. Philadelphia: Fortress, 1985.

Sasson, Jack M. *Jonah*. Anchor Bible 24B. New York: Doubleday, 1990.

Sayers, Dorothy. *The Man Born to Be King: A Play-Cycle on the Life of our Lord and Saviour Jesus Christ*. London: Victor Gollancz, 1943.

Schapiro, James. *A Year in the Life of William Shakespeare: 1599*. London: Faber and Faber / New York: Harper Collins, 2005.

Schleiermacher, Friedrich. *F. Schleiermacher: Hermeneutik. Nach den Handschriften neu herausgegeben und eingeleitet*, Heinz Kimmerle, ed. 2nd ed. C. Winter: Heidelberg, 1974. ET: *Friedrich Schleiermacher: Hermeneutics: The Handwritten Manuscripts*, Heinz Kimmerle, ed., James Duke and Jack Forstman, transl. Missoula, Montana: Scholars, 1977.

Schweitzer, Albert. *Von Reimarus zu Wrede*. 1906. ET: *The Quest of the Historical Jesus*. W. Montgomery, transl. 1910.

Sesboüé, Bernard. *L'évangile et la Tradition*. Paris: Bayard, 2008. ET: *Gospel and Tradition*, Patricia Kelly, transl. Miami: Convivium, 2012.

Shakespeare, William. *Hamlet*. 1599. Texts in Ann Thompson and Neil Taylor, *Hamlet* 2 vols. London: Arden Shakespeare, 2006.

———. *The Tempest*. c.1611. Text in Alden T. Vaughan and Virginia Mason Vaughan, *The Tempest*. London: Arden Shakespeare, 2011.

Shapiro, James. *Contested Will: Who Wrote Shakespeare?* New York: Simon and Schuster, 2010.

Shiell, William D. *Delivering from Memory: The Effect of Performance on the Early Christian Audience*. Eugene, Ore: Pickwick Publications, 2011.

Steiner, George. *After Babel*. Oxford: Oxford University Press, 1975.

———. *Real Presences*. London: Faber and Faber, 1989.

Steinmetz, David. "The Superiority of Pre-Critical Exegesis." In *Theology Today* **37** (1980): 27–38; also in *Ex auditu* **1** (1985): 74–82.

Theissen, Gerd, and Annette Merz, *The Historical Jesus: A Comprehensive Guide*. Philadelphia: Fortress, 1998.

Topel, L. John, S. J., "Faith, Exegesis, and Theology." In *Irish Theological Quarterly* **69** (2004): 337–48.

Trimble, Michael R. *The Soul in the Brain: The Cerebral Basis of Language, Art, and Belief.* Baltimore: Johns Hopkins, 2007.

Tyrrell, George. *Christianity at the Crossroads.* London and New York: Longmans, Green and Company, 1910.

Vermes, Geza. *Jesus the Jew: A Historian's Reading of the Gospels.* London: Collins, 1973.

Victorine Texts in Translation: Exegesis, Theology and Spirituality from the Abbey of St Victor, 3, Interpretation of Scripture: Theory. Franklin T. Harkins and Frans van Liere, eds. Turnhout, Belgium: Brepols, 2012.

Wainwright, Geoffrey. "Towards an Ecumenical Hermeneutic: How Can All Christians Read the Scriptures Together?" In *Gregorianum* **76** (1995): 648–49.

Walker, Adrian. "Fundamentalism and the Catholicity of Truth." In *Communio* **29** (2002) 5–27.

Williams, Charles. *The Place of the Lion.* London: Victor Gollancz, 1931.

Wolf, Maryanne. *Proust and the Squid.* New York: HarperCollins, 2007.

Wright, N. T. *Christian Origins and the Question of God, 1. The New Testament and the People of God.* London: SPCK, 1992.

———. *Jesus and the Victory of God.* London: S.P.C.K. / Minneapolis: Fortress, 1996.

INDEX OF AUTHORS AND SOURCES